Supporting Children with
Co-ordination Difficulties

Hull Learning Services

David Fulton Publishers

David Fulton Publishers Ltd
The Chiswick Centre, 414 Chiswick High Road, London W4 5TF

www.fultonpublishers.co.uk
www.onestopeducation.co.uk

David Fulton Publishers is a division of Granada Learning Limited, part of ITV plc.

BK
$16.91

British Library Cataloguing in Publication Data
A catalogue record for this book is available from the British Library.

ISBN 1 84312 227 8

Typeset by Matrix Creative, Wokingham
Printed and bound in Great Britain

Contents

Foreword

This book was written by members of the Education Service for Physical Disability, based in Hull:

Susan Coulter
Lesley Kynman
Elizabeth Morling

with thanks to senior adviser John Hill for his support and encouragement throughout.

It is one of a series of eleven titles providing an up-to-date overview of special educational needs (SEN) for special educational needs co-ordinators (SENCOs), teachers and other professionals, and parents.

The books were produced in response to training and information needs raised by teachers, support staff and parents in Hull. The aim of these books is to raise awareness of and address many of the issues involved in creating inclusive environments.

For details of other titles and how to order, please see page 133.

Acknowledgements

With grateful thanks to:

Anny Bibby (educational psychologist);
Carol Ogden (SENCO);
Sue Marris (SENCO);
Jackie Picoss (SENCO);

Mrs Gilson, and the pupils of Priory Primary School for their drawings for the visual timetables. Also to Isaac, Rosie and Darren, for acting as our models.

Introduction

This book is intended to support teachers in the development of children's motor co-ordination skills. The approach used recognises that the acquisition of gross motor skills underpins the development of fine motor and independence skills. The term 'co-ordination difficulty' has been used in preference to dyspraxia or developmental co-ordination disorder in recognition that many children will have difficulties which have not been diagnosed or labelled.

Research suggests that between 5 and 6 per cent of the school population will have motor co-ordination difficulties, to a greater or lesser degree, arising from dyspraxia. Add to this figure the children who have motor co-ordination difficulties associated with dyslexia, attention deficit hyperactivity disorder (ADHD), autistic spectrum disorders and difficulties resulting from medical conditions such as cerebral palsy, hyper-mobility syndromes and developmental delays, and the percentage of affected children increases.

> *"On current evidence it seems that at least a quarter, and perhaps one third or more of the population is likely to be affected to at least some degree by one or more of these conditions."*

(Richardson 2001)

It is likely that every teacher in a primary school will be able to identify several children in his/her class who experience difficulties with motor planning and co-ordination skills.

The Special Educational Needs and Disability Act 2001 (SENDA) states that all teachers are teachers of children with SEN. It also states that teachers' planning should be flexible in order to recognise the needs of all children as individuals and to ensure progression, relevance and differentiation (SEN CoP 2001, 5.2 and 5.19).

It is anticipated that users of this book will 'dip into' sections relating to their area of concern. However, it is important to read the sections on 'Making sense of the senses' and 'Understanding physical development' to gain an awareness of the underlying processes involved.

Current teaching styles acknowledge multiple intelligences, understanding that children learn in different ways. Some are visual learners, others may be auditory learners while many respond to kinaesthetic experiences. A multi-sensory approach is recommended wherever appropriate. Activities are suggested which can be adapted to the developmental stage of the child.

Reference
Richardson, A.J. http://www.scre.ac.uk/forum/forum2001/richardson.html

Part 1

An overview of co-ordination difficulties

Making sense of the senses

A child with motor co-ordination difficulties presents as being inattentive and clumsy, sometimes failing to make the academic progress that one suspects he/she is capable of. Parents and teachers can be puzzled as to the reasons for this behaviour. To understand the causes of this type of developmental difficulty one must look at the way in which the senses work together to influence learning.

There are three main senses which need to work effectively together to allow us to experience, interpret and respond to stimuli in our environment. This process is known as **sensory integration**.

1. Sense of touch (tactile)

The tactile system sends information to the brain, via cells in the skin. This information includes light touch, pain, temperature and pressure. It is this sense which enables us to rummage in a bag to find a pen or a coin without looking.

When the tactile system is not working properly, a child may hate to be cuddled, dislike getting his/her hands dirty or avoid playing with certain textures. He/she may also be sensitive to particular textures in clothing and refuse to eat certain 'textured' foods. The child may be unable to moderate his/her own touch, resulting in rough play, sometimes misinterpreted by others as aggression.

The term 'tactile defensiveness' is used to describe a condition where a child is extremely sensitive to the lightest of touches.

When the tactile system is immature, abnormal neural signals are sent to the cortex in the brain, which can interfere with other brain processes. (The cortex is the part of the brain that interprets information.) This interference can lead to the brain being overstimulated, which results in the person having difficulties organising, concentrating and dealing with physical contact with others.

2. Sense of movement (vestibular)

The vestibular system uses structures in the inner ear to detect movement and changes in the position of your head. It enables us to remain upright, to adjust our position, to balance and to interpret movement. The vestibular system helps to maintain muscle tone, co-ordinate the two sides of the body (bilateral co-ordination) and holds the head up against gravity. When the vestibular system is working effectively, a child can look up at the board then return to a book without losing his/her place. He/she can balance on one leg for long enough to kick a ball.

Immaturities in the vestibular system can be seen in two ways: hyper-reaction and hypo-reaction, over- and under-reaction respectively. Some children are hypersensitive to vestibular stimulation and may be frightened of ordinary movements, e.g. using slides, swings, steps and slopes. They may also be apprehensive about walking on uneven or unstable surfaces, e.g. gravel paths or sandy beaches. The child who reacts like this can appear to be fearful in open spaces, e.g. when in the gym or hall. The other extreme is a child who seeks intense sensory experiences by twirling, jumping and spinning in order to stimulate the vestibular system.

3. Sense of position (proprioceptive)

When a person moves, (proprioceptive) signals are sent from the muscles, tendons and joints to the brain to enable us to know what our body is doing. The proprioceptive system could be described as an internal sense of vision. It enables us to carry out actions without having to look, e.g. fastening the top button of a shirt or putting on a jumper over the head.

When the proprioceptive system is not working correctly, a child may appear clumsy, fall often, have limited understanding of his/her position in space, bump into furniture or brush along the wall when walking in a corridor. The child may have difficulties handling small objects, leading to problems with independence skills and fine motor skills.

Another aspect of proprioception is 'praxis' or motor planning. This is the ability to plan and execute motor tasks. This is essential to learning new skills.

In summary, sensory integration takes place in the following way:

- **Input** – information from the sensory system goes into the brain via sensory pathways.
- **Processing** – the information from the senses is processed and sent to other centres within the brain where it is 'made sense of' and translated into perception and learning. This is a two-way journey with information being sent back to the sensory systems to enable modification of movement and behaviour.
- **Output** – the brain then enables the child to carry out integrated actions, e.g. movements, interaction and functions.

When there is a problem in processing information from one of the sensory systems, the result can be poor functioning in a number of areas as all of the sensory pathways are interconnected.

References

East Riding Community Healthcare (undated) *Developmental Coordination Disorder*.

Wright, Sally (June 1989) *Physiotherapy: Applied to the Treatment of the Child with Dyspraxia*, Dyspraxia Trust.

Understanding physical development

Once an understanding has been established of how the sensory systems work together to allow the child to interact with his/her environment, the stages of normal physical development need to be considered. An understanding of these stages may help teachers prioritise areas of skill development. Age-referenced stages of normal development in the areas of gross motor, fine motor and independence skills precede the relevant sections.

Normal growth and development

1. Motor skills develop in a cephalo-caudal direction (head to toe). The baby gains head control, then shoulder control before gaining pelvis stability, walking and controlled hand skills.	**2. Control or core stability** is gained in a proximal-distal direction (starting with joints nearest the body – leading to those furthest away). A child learns to control the shoulders, then the elbows, followed by wrists and finally hands and fingers.	**3. Fine motor control** develops in a medial-distal direction (from the midline outwards).

4. A child's early movements involve the whole body; the child then learns to separate (disassociate) movements.

He/she learns to reach for an object first with the whole body:
- then with two arms;
- then with one;
- then learns to grasp an object;
- later learns to release the object.

Reference

Klein, M.D. (1982) *Pre-Writing Skills: Skill Starters for Motor Development*, Communication Skill Builders.

Identifying children with co-ordination difficulties

The table below is intended to help teachers build up a profile of the child who is experiencing motor co-ordination difficulties. Possible difficulties have been categorised into the stage in which they are typically seen. It should be noted that children in Key Stages 1 and 2 are likely to experience some of the difficulties listed in the Foundation Stage section. Similarly, some pupils in Key Stages 3 and 4 will experience difficulties from earlier Key Stages. Corresponding sections of the book provide classroom strategies which can be used to target specific areas of development. Appendix 2 provides pro-formas for a Pupil Profile.

Area of development	Possible difficulties seen at the Foundation Stage
Sensory	<ul><li>very excitable, making shrill or loud noises, hand flapping;</li><li>cannot sit still during circle or story time;</li><li>limited concentration, flitting from one activity to another;</li><li>distressed by high levels of noise;</li><li>dislikes being touched or avoids certain textures;</li><li>fiddles, chews objects or clothes;</li><li>poor safety awareness or a fear of heights;</li><li>fussy eater.</li></ul>
Gross motor skills	<ul><li>clumsy movements, bumps into objects, falls, trips;</li><li>easily knocked off-balance;</li><li>difficulty climbing on a small climbing frame;</li><li>difficulty getting into or onto play equipment and chairs;</li><li>jumps from inappropriate heights with no sense of danger;</li><li>has to squat to pick up toys from the floor;</li><li>difficulty getting up from the floor without using hands;</li><li>difficulty jumping with both feet together;</li><li>difficulty pedalling a tricycle;</li><li>climbs the stairs leading with one foot;</li><li>difficulty throwing, catching and kicking a large ball.</li></ul>
Fine motor skills	<ul><li>uncertain of hand dominance;</li><li>avoids jigsaws and construction toys;</li><li>poor pencil grip;</li><li>unable to use scissors;</li><li>struggles to build tower of six one-inch cubes.</li></ul>

Independence skills	<ul><li>difficulty taking off coat and hanging it on a peg;</li><li>struggles with undressing;</li><li>unable to use the toilet independently;</li><li>messy eater, prefers to finger-feed;</li><li>spills drinks.</li></ul>
Communication	<ul><li>plays alone, rather than in a group;</li><li>lack of imaginative play;</li><li>difficulty following simple routines and instructions;</li><li>unclear speech, cannot speak in sentences;</li><li>avoidance of eye contact.</li></ul>
Area of development	**Possible difficulties seen at Key Stages 1 and 2**
Sensory	<ul><li>easily distracted, lacks persistence;</li><li>unable to use space effectively in PE or playground;</li><li>difficulty judging distance and direction;</li><li>difficulty sitting still;</li><li>dislikes being touched;</li><li>can be rough in play without realising;</li><li>irrational fear of open space or heights;</li><li>poor self-image, attention-seeking behaviour, withdrawn, underactive, reluctant to participate;</li><li>lacks inhibition;</li><li>poor visual tracking;</li><li>difficulty copying from the board;</li><li>dribbles from mouth.</li></ul>
Gross motor skills	<ul><li>awkward, clumsy, bumps into people and objects;</li><li>difficulty hopping, jumping, skipping;</li><li>poor balance;</li><li>poor ball skills;</li><li>difficulty learning new tasks or sequences.</li></ul>
Fine motor skills	<ul><li>poor sitting posture;</li><li>uncertain of hand dominance;</li><li>immature pencil grasp and poor pencil control;</li><li>poor drawing skills, messy when using paints;</li><li>difficulty using scissors;</li><li>avoids handwriting tasks;</li><li>difficulty setting out work in books;</li><li>unable to construct a model following a diagram or plan.</li></ul>
Independence skills	<ul><li>slow, messy eater;</li><li>slow to change for PE, mixes up order and orientation of clothes;</li><li>avoids using the toilet at school.</li></ul>

Communication	• poor eye contact; • daydreams; • poor articulation, difficulties organising speech; • slow to process information and give feedback (verbal or physical); • develops avoidance strategies; • asks never-ending questions.
Organisation	• unable to remember messages; • forgets, cannot find dinner money; PE equipment • cannot cope with changes of routine; • difficulty selecting equipment for a lesson or activity; • poor sequencing skills.
Area of development	**Possible difficulties seen at Key Stages 3 and 4**
Sensory	• low self-esteem; • little sense of personal safety; • poor road sense as a pedestrian or cyclist; • difficulty coping with board work in class.
Gross motor skills	• difficulty in PE and games activities; • reluctant to participate in team games; • evidence of motor stereotypes such as hand-flapping.
Fine motor skills	• difficulty keeping up with written work; • books are untidy with work being difficult to read and mark; • short written responses which do not match verbal ability; • unable to manipulate ruler, compass, protractor; • struggles in practical subjects.
Independence skills	• avoids removing jumper/sweatshirt in very hot weather; • avoids eating with cutlery; • personal hygiene lacks attention.
Communication	• unable to follow complex instructions; • difficulty sequencing events, particularly in written format; • poor speech production; • socially isolated; • preoccupied with topics or subjects.
Organisation	• carries all belongings for fear of forgetting something; • loses books and writing equipment; • has an unkempt appearance; • encroaches into his/her neighbour's personal space.

Overlapping conditions

Pupils with any of the conditions mentioned below will have some overlap in the difficulties experienced (listed centrally). Conditions may also co-exist. Based on the statistics in the Introduction there might be 5–8 pupils in the average class with a mix of problems, having educational implications which require action.

Global delay
Core feature:
- delay in all areas of development.

Additionally, these pupils may experience difficulties in some of the following areas:

Sensory
Sensitivity to touch/noise/light;
Visual/auditory perception;
Concentration/attention control.

Gross motor skills
Balance and co-ordination;
Playing team games involving specific skill levels/rules.

Fine motor skills
Hand-dominance;
Handwriting/note-taking;
Using scissors/tools, etc.

Independence skills
Eating/dressing, etc.

Communication
Play skills;
Speech difficulties;
Self-esteem/eye contact;
Social skills.

Organisation skills
Setting out number/work;
Remembering instructions;
Negotiating the school site.

Dyspraxia
Core features:
- poor motor co-ordination and planning;
- difficulties with personal organisation.

Dyslexia
Core features:
- difficulties at word level despite intervention;
- weak visual processing skills.

Asperger's syndrome
Core features:
- difficulties with communication and social interaction;
- impaired imagination;
- rigidity of behaviour.

ADHD
Core features:
- difficulties with attention and concentration;
- very impulsive;
- hyperactivity.

Medical conditions
Hypermobility syndromes (Ehlers-Danlos, Marfan's, etc.), Down's syndrome; lax joints and low muscle tone are key features.

Pupil profiling

Having a clear idea of a pupil's strengths and weaknesses will inform both teaching and learning styles.

It is not always necessary to have a diagnosis of a pupil's condition to be able to move forward. There may be differing professional opinions or possibly overlapping conditions, which may be identified as the pupil progresses through school and difficulties become more apparent. However, the teacher's approach should always be the same. Identify the problems experienced by the pupil and put appropriate intervention strategies in place where possible.

A Pupil Profile will establish a *baseline* of the pupil's abilities in core development areas, which in turn will help to identify:

- appropriate strategies for moving forward in each area;
- how the environment can be structured to suit the pupil's needs;
- when outside agencies or support services should be consulted.

Use the Appendix 2 checklists to form a profile of the pupil's abilities, and checklists within other areas of the book to gather more detailed information.

Ensure that the pupil's strengths are also noted, e.g.:

- many are competent with computers and approach them intuitively;
- many are verbally able and can relate imaginative stories;
- out-of-school interests may highlight noticeable strengths in one area of the curriculum, e.g. natural history.

Additionally, use information about 'multiple intelligences' to find out which are the pupil's main modes of learning and try to teach through these.

As the pupil gets older, teach coping strategies and organisational skills, which can be applied throughout adult life.

Remember that pupils do not progress evenly in all areas. It is quite natural for them to move forward in different areas at different speeds.

NB: Some strategies recur in different areas of this book since they address a number of different needs, e.g. the use of cue cards supports:

- independent work skills;
- problems with short-term memory;
- auditory difficulties;
- communication difficulties.

The Graduated Response

This chapter considers how the special needs of children with co-ordination difficulties may be met within the Graduated Response required by the SEN Code of Practice 2001. Schools are expected to use a range of strategies within a cycle of continual and systematic planning, teaching and assessing before involving outside agencies.

Professional development

Some teachers and teaching assistants may perceive that they lack the necessary skills and knowledge to support children with co-ordination difficulties. It is likely that individual staff will identify their own professional development training needs, e.g. accessing children to the PE curriculum, assessing handwriting skills, promoting independent learning. From here the professional development co-ordinator will be able to address whole-school training issues, by organising INSET, which focuses on the areas in which teachers and teaching assistants feel least secure.

School approach

Through experience and sharing of good practice it is possible to formulate a whole-school approach to meeting the needs of children with co-ordination difficulties.

Resource bank

Schools may wish to build up a resource bank of cue cards, visual timetables, differentiated PE activities which can be used as starting points to support these children.

Planning, teaching and assessing

It should be noted that, on the whole, the strategies suggested in this book are derived from good classroom practice. In the Foundation Stage these activities can be incorporated into existing learning experiences, providing a suitably differentiated curriculum which will support the physical development of most children. If concerns arise about the progress of an individual child, these should be discussed with the parents and appropriate intervention agreed as part of the ongoing cycle of planning, teaching and assessing. In later Key Stages, where a concern has been noted about the progress of an individual pupil, interventions required may be additional to or different from activities offered to other pupils. In these cases the child will be included on the 'School Action' list and an Individual Education Plan (IEP) devised by the teacher and SENCO. At each stage the parents, and where appropriate the child, should be involved in the target setting process.

Involvement of health professionals

Some children arrive in school with a specific medical diagnosis with associated co-ordination difficulties, e.g. Down's syndrome, Marfan's syndrome or autistic spectrum disorder. There can be no hard and fast rule as to when children with co-ordination difficulties should be referred to health professionals. Evidence collected through the graduated approach to meeting SEN may, in time, indicate a need for referral to a relevant health professional such as the occupational therapy service or physiotherapy service. Referrals are usually made by the GP at the parents' request; in some cases, the school doctor will refer children with the parents' permission.

The Graduated Response to motor co-ordination difficulties

Graduated Response	Trigger	Intervention
The differentiated curriculum	Inadequate progress noted due to: • limited concentration; • delayed gross and fine motor skills; • poor independence skills; • unclear speech.	• provide a wide range of differentiated activities; • discuss concerns with parents; • interventions agreed with parents; • ongoing teacher assessment; • evidence of inadequate progress is collected.
School Action If progress is made at this stage, return to the differentiated curriculum prior to School Action	Continued inadequate progress in the areas of weakness identified above, resulting in: • inability to access the whole curriculum.	• IEP (plus continued differentiation); • extra teacher and teaching assistant time; • additional specialist equipment; • specialist staff development/training opportunities; • one-off or occasional assessment and/or advice from LEA services.
School Action Plus If progress is made at this stage, return to School Action	• Evidence of a sensory or physical need requiring specialist equipment and/or regular advice and visits from LEA or NHS services.	• IEP (plus continued differentiation); • extra teacher and teaching assistant time; • additional equipment; • specialist staff development/training; • sustained support from LEA services; • involvement of relevant medical personnel, e.g. occupational therapist/ physiotherapist.
Statement If progress at this stage, return to School Action Plus when appropriate	• sensory and/or physical needs continue to severely restrict curriculum access; • continued inadequate progress.	• as above; plus request for statutory assessment.

Individual Education Plans

Strategies to enable the pupil to progress should be recorded in an Individual Education Plan (IEP). Some considerations should be made when devising IEPs:

- The IEP should include information about:
  - short-term targets set for or by the pupil;
  - teaching strategies to be used;
  - provision to be put in place;
  - when the plan is to be reviewed;
  - success and/or exit criteria;
  - outcomes (to be recorded when the IEP is reviewed, CoP 2001).
- For pupils where motor co-ordination difficulties are an element of or the whole of their profile, use identified areas from the Pupil Profile (Appendix 2) when devising his/her IEP. Targets may address priorities from the following areas:
  - sensory development;
  - gross motor skills;
  - fine motor/recording skills;
  - independence skills;
  - communication skills;
  - organisational skills.
- The IEP should only record that which is additional to/different from differentiation already taking place in the classroom.
- The pupil should take part in the target setting and review process where possible.
- Parents should also be included in the target setting and review process, and encouraged to support targets at home. They should be given copies of the IEP.
- Three or four targets should be included in the IEP.
- IEPs should be composed and reviewed at least twice a year.
- Pupils in Early Years settings will need targets to be reviewed at least four times a year and kept continually under review.
- Targets should be achievable, measurable and relevant to the pupil. If pupils are not achieving by the time of review, targets may be too difficult and need breaking down.
- It may be relevant to incorporate programmes into the IEP from health professionals, e.g. occupational therapist, speech and language therapist, physiotherapist.

The following pages give pen pictures of pupils with a range of difficulties and corresponding IEPs to address their needs.

Pen picture (KS1)

Alan	Strategies
Alan is six years old. He has specific learning difficulties and problems with gross and fine motor skills.	*Look in the following:* Classroom organisation: seating position in class (page 23).
Alan has had speech therapy for a number of years. In school he has support from SENSS in a small group once a week, and support from a class assistant (funded from the school's devolved SEN budget) to support foundation and listening skills. He is at School Action Plus of the CoP.	Developing attention and listening skills (page 38).
Generally his teacher describes his gross motor movements as resembling 'a sackful of puppies'. He always has his shirt hanging out, shoes on the wrong feet and has problems putting on his coat.	Developing dressing skills (page 88).
Alan says that he does not like sitting still. He is distractible, always moving and his attention flits from one thing to another in swift succession. When with an adult Alan gives a constant running commentary of his observations.	Classroom organisation: keeping hands busy (page 23).
Writing is large and poorly formed with erratic spacing and many reversals of letters. Alan has significant difficulties copying simple shapes, in particular those involving diagonals, and does not have the patience to look carefully before he executes a copy.	Handwriting remediation (page 63). Fine and gross motor skills crossing the midline (pages 46 and 56). Alternative recording strategies (page 76) and Developing keyboard skills (page 78).
His drawings are idiosyncratic; people have completely irregular body shapes, with legs like ladders or a single solid oblong.	Developing body image (page 118).
Although Alan has learned to run, he does so with flat feet with arms held high. He can jump but not hop. Alan is able to catch a large ball with extended arms and throw two-handed.	Gross motor skill development programme (page 42).
Although skills are relatively poor, confidence is not affected and Alan is very willing to persevere with activities in an effort to improve performance.	

School

School Action Plus

Name: Alan	DOB: 19.03.97
Date: 8.9.03	Review date: 1.11.03

Nature of pupil's difficulties: Alan has co-ordination difficulties:
- poor letter formation, many reversals of letters, unable to produce letters with diagonals;
- poor gross motor skills, unable to hop, walk on tiptoes or balance on one leg for longer than one second;
- poor body image, unable to put shoes on correct feet.

Targets	Strategies	Resources	Evaluation
Handwriting To complete 'Write from the Start' booklet 4A (focus on orientation). To be able to cross the midline of his body.	• complete worksheet 3 times a week • in PE play 'Hokey-Cokey' and 'Pass the Hot Potato' in a ring • 'Simon says…' actions involving opposite sides of the body • cross-dancing from Brain Gym	• book 1, booklet 4A, Ultra pencil grip • PE equipment	
Keyboard skills To type his first name on the computer.	• practise typing for 10 minutes a day. Print out results as a reward.	• drill and rote typing programme	
Gross motor skills To balance on one leg for 3 seconds (using small-steps programme provided).	• marching practice in PE gradually raising knees higher and using slower tempo music • climb in and out of hoops	• tape recorder and music in different rhythms • hoops	
Independence skills To put shoes on the correct feet.	• put red stickers on the instep of both shoes and instruct Alan to 'put the stickers together' before putting them on	• red stickers	

Parental involvement: Parents to continue dressing objective routinely and record progress. Reward for success.

15

Pen picture (KS2)

Sam	Strategies
Sam is eight years old. His milestones had been delayed and a Griffiths test was carried out when he was eight months old because he was not sitting and did not crawl.	*Look in the following:*
Sam likes to walk close to the wall when moving around school.	Making sense of the senses: sense of position (page 4).
He finds it hard to skip and jump and has found it very difficult to learn to swim.	Gross motor skills (page 39).
Sam's writing is a mixture of printing and joined script; his teacher said it has greatly improved since he started joined writing. He forms letters incorrectly and finds it difficult to space words. His writing deteriorates in quality if he is doing a long piece of work.	Visual perception (page 37). Alternative recording strategies (page 76).
Sam is a willing and hard-working child; however, his performance is variable. He finds maths difficult, he can rote learn, e.g. tables, but finds it difficult to solve problems and to complete tasks requiring sequencing and ordering.	Maths (page 26).
He appears to 'switch off' for short periods of time when listening to class input.	Attention and listening skills (page 38).
Sam's organisational skills are poor. He finds it difficult to remember notes/homework, etc. At present this is remedied by close co-operation between Mum and his class teacher. He finds it extremely difficult to follow class instructions and organise himself to complete a task.	Organisational skills (page 120).
Sam finds it difficult to dress himself successfully; he puts trousers on inside out and back to front, socks on with the heel at the top, shoes on the wrong feet.	Dressing skills (page 88).
Sam still finds it impossible to use a knife and fork, resorting to a spoon or fingers; he also becomes very messy in the process.	Eating skills (page 89).

Name: Sam	DOB: 09.09.96
Date: 15.9.04	Review date: 03.12.04

Nature of pupil's difficulties: Sam has developmental co-ordination disorder:
- difficulties producing a longer piece of writing which has a pleasing appearance;
- difficulties dressing after PE;
- difficulties sequencing events for a story.

Targets	Strategies	Resources	Evaluation
To size letters correctly when writing a short piece of work.	• use of 'Write from the Start' programme on daily basis • use of paper with extra lines to indicate the correct size of letters • daily practice using school handwriting scheme	• 'Write from the Start' booklet 4C • adult oversight • handwriting practice paper with guidelines (LDA)	
To put jumper on with correct orientation after PE.	• teach how to take off jumper and lay it out on the desk ready to put back on • teach how to put arms in first and pull over head	• adult support before and after PE	
To sequence 5 pictures about an event.	• sequencing pictures/photographs of everyday activities, visits • sequencing ideas for story writing in picture form prior to writing	• LDA cards • digital camera • proforma for story layout, prepared pictures to sequence	

Parental involvement: Encourage laying out clothes at home. Recalling events after an outing.

Pen picture (KS3)

James	Strategies
James is a Year 8 pupil who was diagnosed with developmental co-ordination disorder/dyspraxia. He has been assessed by the Occupational Therapy Service and given coping strategies. OT intervention was not recommended.	*Look in the following:*
James is a pupil of average ability who has struggled throughout school with his written work. James has always been slightly clumsy, but masked this in the primary school by 'clowning around'. In the secondary school, James stumbles a lot. He tends to bump into furniture in the classroom and bumps into walls unless focused on looking where he's going. James can be unsteady when bending to get his books out of his bag. He has been known to nearly miss his chair when sitting down, resulting in embarrassment when other pupils laugh. James is constantly fidgeting. This is often irritating for other pupils and distracting for teachers, which leads to James being told off.	Organising PE sessions: spatial problems (page 36). Making sense of the senses: sense of position (page 4). Attention and listening skills (page 38).
James frequently arrives at lessons with a just a pencil stub or a biro refill in his pencil case; he says he has lots of equipment at home but never remembers to put it in his bag. He also carries all of his books with him all the time, explaining that this is the way he makes sure he never forgets anything.	Preparing for secondary transfer (page 101). Classroom organisation (page 23).
James's handwriting ranges from being legible on a good day to untidy and barely legible on another. Teachers' comments reveal that they expect James to be able to produce his best writing all the time. James's work is generally poorly presented with untidy corrections and inaccurate use of a ruler. His letter formation is correct although he has difficulties writing on a line. James struggles to copy from the board, but he can write to dictation, although it is usually very difficult to read his notes. James has tried word processing his work on the computer but is frustrated because his keyboard skills are very slow.	Visual perception (page 37). Developing keyboard skills (page 78).
Four men and a jolly boy came out of the black and pink house quickly to see the bright violet sun, but the sun was behind a cloud. *Four men and a jolly boy came out of the black and pink house quickly to see the bright violet sun, but the sun was behind a cloud.*	
Word processing speed 26 letters per minute, handwriting speed 44 letters per minute (average 75).	

School

School Action Plus

| Name: James | DOB: 24.03.90 |
| Date: 15.03.04 | Review date: June 2004 |

Nature of pupil's difficulties: James has developmental co-ordination disorder (dyspraxia):

- has difficulties copying from the board;
- is left-handed and struggles to produce consistently legible handwriting;
- fidgets constantly;
- poor organisational skills.

Targets	Strategies	Resources	Evaluation
To minimise peer conflict caused by constant fidgeting and arm conflict.	• to sit in the centre of the classroom, towards the front • to be provided with a piece of Blu-tack or similar to enable 'quiet' fiddling which will not disturb others • to sit to the left of right-handers	• seating plan • Blu-tack	
To improve keyboard skills as an alternative recording strategy – improve speed in letters per minute to 40.	• daily practice using a structured small-step programme • speed test repeated fortnightly to plot progress	• Penso, Dorothy, *Word Processing Skills for Pupils with Co-ordination Difficulties* • access to computer/word processor • 10 minutes' daily practice	
To be equipped with the correct books and equipment for each lesson.	• organise books and equipment into subject areas • pack school bag before bedtime • put things back into the subject folder after use • teachers complete record card	• homework diary/Dictaphone • colour-coded timetable • clear plastic wallets • duplicate writing equipment into each wallet • record sheet	

Parental involvement: Parents will check the school bag each evening.

The pupils' perspective

The CoP states that *"Children and young people with special educational needs and circumstances have their own views about what sort of help they would like to help them make the most of their education."*

The following comments are from pupils with co-ordination difficulties and reflect the difficulties they have encountered in school and the support they have valued.

Some pupils were able to recognise some of their strengths and overcome some of their difficulties through the support they encountered. Ben said confidently: 'I'm good at reading, I'm good at English but find handwriting difficult.' He valued using the computer and said, 'I have typing lessons on a Monday and Friday.'

Jim valued having support: 'Mrs Cook (his CSA) helps me. It's great. We get the coins out then I can do money sums.'

Joe had been taking part in group work, three times a week, to improve gross motor skills and said: 'It's getting better, you remember what it used to be like, I'm getting better at PE.'

Tim felt that things had got better: 'I've got my laptop now, I sit and get on with it.' He was getting better results because the presentation of his work was improved, which, in turn, was making him feel more positive about himself.

Some comments were less positive. One pupil described various negative experiences that still affected his confidence and coloured his views of school. He made comments like: 'It's hard… they shout at me… I have to stay in.'

Stuart said: 'Everything is hard… nobody helps me… I get into trouble.' Stuart was observed as having a difficult time at school. He was increasingly in trouble and was losing the confidence to tackle any new task. He was having tummy ache because he did not want to go to school.

It is hoped that the suggestions in this book will help to support pupils appropriately, thus avoiding the negative experiences described above.

Home–school partnership

Parents play a major part in the support of their children; this can be enhanced by a good home–school partnership, which also includes any other professionals who may be involved, e.g. occupational therapists, physiotherapists.

Strategies to help to create a good partnership:

- Parental concerns about issues should be listened to and addressed.
- In the Early Years parents and teachers may together note a child's difficulties to create a profile of the child's strengths and weaknesses.
- Some parents may see the results of anxiety and pressure, reflected in their children's behaviour at home, to which there may be simple solutions.
- It may be necessary to find joint solutions to issues such as eating school lunches, length of time on homework, difficulties in following instructions appropriately.
- Parents should be encouraged to share information and/or relevant reports from professionals about their child with school staff, where this would help to develop a complete picture of the child.
- School should also ensure that they, in turn, inform parents of visits from professionals and pass on any relevant information or reports.
- Parents should be involved in the IEP process and a part of supporting targets set.
- It would be useful to encourage participation in activities which the child enjoys, and follow subjects at option times in which they find success, in order to boost self-esteem.
- Schools can help by using a home/school diary as a means of a two-way communication process to pass on relevant information, as the pupil may have difficulties in remembering/organising.
- Teachers and parents should be sensitive to the child by not discussing his/her difficulties in his/her hearing.
- As children make transitions between schools, discussions will be important between parents, staff from the receiving school and the school that the child is leaving. This will enable knowledge of the pupil to be passed on and strategies to be put in place, to give appropriate support in the new school.
- Endeavour to pass on positive comments to parents and avoid other children making negative comments by 'telling tales'.

NB: Parents can be given handouts (see Appendix 6) in order to help their children develop gross motor skills, and support the development of organisational skills and independent dressing skills.

General school issues

For any pupil with an overlapping condition in which co-ordination difficulties are a core feature there are implications for management which will need consideration and forward-planning.

On-site mobility checklist:

- Are there any stairs without handrails?
- Is the pupil safe on the stairs or is adult support required to ensure safety?
- Are corridors free of clutter?
- Are there any sunken mat wells that could be a trip hazard?
- Can all pupils open doors independently? Check strength of automatic door closers and have them re-adjusted if there is a problem.
- Do fire doors open easily?
- Is there a clear path around classrooms for pupils to negotiate?
- If the pupil has a physical management programme, is there somewhere for this to be carried out?
- Can the pupil move from one class to another without getting disorientated?
- Are subject areas clearly marked? It might be helpful to colour-code different areas.

Another primary concern is attitudes to and expectations of pupils, since these inform the ethos of the school and establish a warm, caring environment in which pupils can learn and grow, regardless of the difficulties they experience.

Be aware that some pupils will try to compensate for their problems by becoming the 'class clown' or by demonstrating over-boisterous behaviour, introversion or even depression. This is particularly important in KS2 as they become more aware of their own performance compared to their peers'.

Always have a positive attitude towards pupils:

- Praise whenever possible (emphasise abilities not disabilities).
- Look for strengths or areas of interest.
- Let pupils know you are interested in their difficulties.
- Be aware that pupils may be good verbally but have poor performance skills so accept verbal evidence of attainment and use alternative means of recording (page 76).
- Try to maintain pupils' confidence; never ridicule or compare them with others (see Promoting self-esteem, page 99).
- Be aware that pupils may not be deliberately naughty but simply not *know* how to respond appropriately in a given situation.
- Be constructively critical.
- Be aware of your own attitude to pupils' problems.

Expectations of pupils:

- Have high expectations – do not put pupils into a lower ability group just because performance is poor.
- Establish baselines, e.g. check whether pupils know the alphabet, the days of the week and months of the year in correct sequence; if they can tell the time; check if independence skills are developed, e.g. dressing and eating (page 89).
- Some pupils have great difficulties with numbers (e.g. setting out work, learning number bonds, tables, etc.), reading music or anything involving the interpretation of symbols.
- Others may have difficulties copying/drawing diagrams and may need intervention programmes to develop visual perception/spatial awareness.
- Pupils may tire more easily due to the effort to keep up, and consequently may be inconsistent in day-to-day performance.
- Be aware of the possibility of pupils developing avoidance techniques.
- Set achievable goals and try to improve one area of work at a time.

Classroom organisation – pupil-friendly environments help pupils feel relaxed:

- Aid organisational skills by clearly labelling drawers, etc. – colour-code if easier.
- Provide a quiet area, e.g. a book corner or library with few distractions, to reduce stimulation if necessary.
- Ensure that key words and main points are included in classroom displays for each topic/module.
- Sit pupils at the front of the class so that they have a good view of the board and can focus attention on the teacher – always facing the board, not at an angle to it, since this distorts visual perception.
- Ensure pupils are in a good sitting position for working – at the proper height table, sitting with straight back and feet flat (see page 61).
- If a pupil has difficulties sitting still or is constantly touching things at story time, give him/her something to play with which is fairly discreet, e.g. a piece of Blu-tack, stress ball.

Aid confidence and independent work skills by:

- splitting up work, if possible, into manageable tasks – a 'small-steps' approach makes objectives achievable and builds confidence;
- ensuring written material is visually clear and uncluttered, e.g. break up large blocks of written text into manageable pieces;
- presenting work modules in a multi-sensory format wherever possible;
- putting key words on flashcards/alphabet/number lines, etc. on pupils' desks to provide a visual prompt;
- giving new information more than once and allowing opportunities for overlearning;
- providing cue cards for different activities – if a group would benefit from a similar approach, use a flip chart (NB: a pictorial representation may be more appropriate for younger pupils), e.g. preparation for work in geography:

For this activity you need:

Geography workbook	Pencil	World globe

- providing older pupils with a range of *written* cue cards on a key ring for different objectives/subjects, e.g. to aid presentation:

Name (top left)   Date (top right)

<u>Title centred and underlined</u>

Draw a margin if required.

If answering numbered questions, put the number in the margin.

Leave one/two lines between the answers.

- allowing plenty of time to organise thoughts and complete the task;
- grading pupils on their own performance and progress, not in comparison with the rest of the class;
- ensuring that you have pupils' attention before giving instructions, which should be precise and concise; repeat if necessary;
- building in short breaks for physical activities/games at primary level, e.g. 'Simon Says…', Brain Gym exercises;
- giving plenty of time to copy from the board – remember that each time pupils look away from the board they may have difficulties finding their place again;
- aiding pupils to copy work from the board, by either:
  - using different coloured pens for each line; or
  - writing key words in different coloured pens; or
  - quartering the board so that pupils know which quarter they are copying from;
- drawing a box when a drawing is required to help pupils organise work on a page;
- gearing questions to pupils' level so that they do not fail;
- giving individual help whenever possible;
- encouraging pupils to ask for help when stuck;
- allowing pupils to have water bottles on their desks to maintain energy levels and concentration – this has also been found to be effective in improving behaviour.

Support problems with short-term memory by:

- providing visual cues, e.g. photographs/objects of reference;
- using 'Post-its', e.g. to develop organisational skills;
- providing parents with vocabulary for the next teaching module, so that it can be practised prior to starting work;
- highlighting important points in notes;
- making visual timetables.

Support long-term memory by:

- revisiting work done on a regular basis;
- teaching pupils how to make effective notes – concise, with numbered points and with key words underlined/highlighted;
- helping pupils to plan their revision;
- producing 'mind maps' for each module to give pupils an overview of the work covered.

To support reading:

- Check that the level of reading material is appropriate and read aloud, if necessary.
- Remember that some pupils have difficulties reading small text.
- When reading long words, encourage pupils to divide syllables with a pencil line.
- Help pupils to pronounce words properly by modelling.
- Do not make the pupil read aloud in class if he/she is reluctant.
- If the pupil loses his/her place easily, use a piece of card either above or below the line being read – some pupils benefit from using two L-shaped pieces of card which can focus on individual words.
- Remember that a pupil may be able to read a passage correctly but not understand it.
- Do not give long lists of words to learn in spelling; two or three at a time is more appropriate.
- Some pupils benefit from a structured spelling programme which has small-step objectives and gives rewards for achievement, e.g. 'Toe by Toe', 'An Eye for Spelling', 'Starspell', etc. (page 130).

Curricular considerations

If there are concerns about safety in the following subjects and areas, ask the SENCO to arrange a risk assessment to ensure safe guidelines are set out and adhered to – this may have staffing implications or require school management decisions. If necessary, include these guidelines in the pupil's IEP.

Specific considerations

Science/D&T/Art:

- With some pupils care will need to be taken in those subjects involving the manipulation of tools and equipment to compensate for poor co-ordination, e.g.:

- – use clamps/test tube racks in science;
- – use clamps or a vice in D&T to ensure stability and best working position;
- – use a mitre saw set to stabilise wood when sawing;
- – ask the school technician to make minor adaptations to tools to improve grip, e.g. extending the handle on a plane;
- – use adapted equipment in food technology, e.g. vegetable workstation, multi-graters, jug blenders, etc. (page 130).
- Use bug boxes/fixed magnifiers, e.g. the QX3 Computer Microscope, which links to the classroom PC and allows greater control over images and magnification.
- Provide chunky crayons/pastels/larger brushes with short handles/decorating brushes, etc. and use non-tip paint pots to support artwork.
- Provide printing stamps to make pictures if pupils lack skills and confidence to draw.
- Allow older pupils to use art/CAD programs to support design modules.
- Use clip art and scanned images to support coursework.
- Provide large bodkins and bigger mesh materials for sewing to support textiles.
- Needle threaders and embroidery hoops might also help.

Maths:
- If pupils have problems developing a counting pattern, provide an abacus for them to use as a counting aid.
- Provide magnetic numbers and a board for initial work to remove the need for writing numbers.
- Allow them to work on the computer to demonstrate understanding of number operations, e.g. '1 to 100', 'Number Shark', etc. to remove the task of writing.
- Stick a number line on pupils' desks or a 100 number square, as appropriate, to support number operations.
- Provide a series of maths templates (page 117) for younger pupils to help them establish a pattern to set out number work and place an arrow to show the direction of calculation.
- Encourage the pupil to mark off numbers (with pencil or highlighter pen) to ensure items are not counted twice.
- Provide a coloured acetate window template, which can be moved around the page to assist older pupils to set out maths work.
- Provide adapted equipment, e.g. a flat compass, 'Circle Scribe' and non-slip rulers (make your own by putting small pieces of sticky Dycem onto the back of standard ruler), large-button calculators.

PE:
- Have spare sandshoes, shorts, T-shirts, etc., for those pupils who always forget them.
- If slow to dress afterwards, quickly lay out clothes in the correct order and give him/her a time limit – gradually try to reduce the time by keeping a record and reward improvement.

- If the session involves team games, the teacher should select the teams rather than the pupils, who may leave those with poorer ability to last.
- In team games, place vulnerable pupils in less busy roles and gradually move them up as skills improve.
- Give spot-demonstrations of target activities and give a visual prompt to pupils with poor motor planning.
- Make allowances for pupils with delayed skills when giving instructions by including alternatives, e.g. rather than having to walk along a bench, pupils may *travel* along a bench by walking, crawling, pulling along on his/her stomach, etc.
- Have a range of different sized/textured balls available for throwing and catching activities (see gross motor resources on page 45) and allow the pupil to choose which one to use; some balls move more slowly than others giving pupils time to position themselves/hands correctly – note any tactile defensive response to different textures.
- Allow plenty of time for practising activities, especially if the pupil is motivated to improve skills.
- If there are problems remembering rules in team games, involve parents, so that the pupil can practise at home.

See page 47 for additional planning requirements for small-group sessions.

Homework:
- Give less homework (e.g. shorter essays, or pick out the main points in note form, etc.).
- Make sure that homework instructions are understood by the pupil – it may be necessary to set up a 'buddy system' to check that homework is taken down.
- Alternatively, have homework written on slips of paper to hand out, post it on the school's website or email it to the pupil's home, whichever is the most appropriate.
- Ask parents to read the homework instructions to the pupil.
- Mark written work on content not style.
- Correct only a limited number of mistakes in written work and do not make pupils write it out again.
- Try to include positive comments about work completed.
- Use Post-its on the front of books/worksheets to remind pupils when to hand in homework at primary level; for secondary pupils see page 102.

External exams:
- To ensure that pupils have the opportunity to demonstrate their knowledge to the full, special arrangements may need to be requested for Y2, Y6 and Y9 SATs and GCSE examinations, e.g. time extension, rest breaks, use of ICT, provision of a reader/ amanuensis (teach dictation skills if necessary – page 83), etc.
- Evidence will need to be provided to demonstrate that these special arrangements have been used successfully in the classroom over a period of time.

Support staff: roles and responsibilities

If the pupil requires support from a class assistant, staff involved should:

have a clear understanding of their roles and responsibilities:
- have a knowledge of their job description;
- maintain a professional demeanour with parents;
- be aware of school policies with regard to behaviour, anti-bullying, Child Protection;
- respect the confidentiality of information for all pupils.

be aware of channels of communication within the school:
- ensure that information provided by parents is given to the appropriate member of staff – class teacher, SENCO;
- ensure that recommendations, communications or reports from outside agencies are passed to the teacher and SENCO;
- ensure that information given to parents is with the knowledge of the class teacher;
- ensure that there is a mechanism for disseminating information to support staff about school activities, e.g. daily diary, staffroom noticeboard.

be recognised as valued members of a team:
- participate in the planning and monitoring process.

be encouraged to make use of their personal skills:
- share skills, e.g. ICT, creative skills.

be supported with appropriate ongoing professional development:
- observe and learn from other professionals in school and in other establishments;
- undertake training in school and through external courses.

encourage the pupil's independence at all times by:
- developing work skills;
- independent self-help skills;
- personal organisation.

Support staff: guidelines for working with pupils

Avoid	Instead
Sitting next to the pupil at all times.	Work with other pupils, while keeping an eye on the pupil you are assigned to.
Offering too close an oversight during breaks and lunchtimes.	Encourage interaction with peers, or allow the pupil to be solitary, follow his/her own interests and relax.
Collecting equipment for the pupil or putting it away.	Encourage the pupil to carry this out independently, e.g. ensuring drawers are clearly labelled.
Completing a task for a pupil.	Ensure work is at an appropriate level and is carried out with minimal support (note any support given).
Using language inappropriate to the pupil.	Give short instructions at the pupil's level of development, with visual prompts.
Making unnecessary allowances for the pupil.	Establish what is required using appropriate strategies and have expectations that a task is completed.
Working in cluttered areas.	Provide a clear, predictable learning environment.
Tolerating undesirable behaviour.	Observe the pupil; determine reasons for behaviour and consider if changes can be made.
Making unrealistic demands on the pupil.	Ensure instructions are at the appropriate level and that goals are achievable.
Making decisions for the pupil.	Give the pupil opportunities to develop choice-making skills by providing structure and restricted choices.
Letting the pupil become dependent on his/her support assistant.	Encourage independent behaviour and work.

Part 2

Understanding core skill development

- Sensory issues
- Gross motor skills
- Fine motor skills

Sensory issues

Please read 'Making sense of the senses' first.

In the classroom pupils may exhibit problems in the following areas:
- Over-/undersensitivity to touch/light/sound, e.g.:
  - disliking loud noises/seeking rough play.
- Visual problems including visual tracking, depth perception, visual perception (particularly important for reading and writing), difficulties maintaining eye contact, e.g.:
  - problems judging distances/poor catching skills/not recognising a familiar object from a different perspective (form constancy), poor social interaction skills.
- Problems with auditory perception, e.g.:
  - not hearing a car approaching/not hearing certain sounds within words or missing whole words.
- Poor attention control, e.g.:
  - not paying attention when instructions are being given, not staying on-task.

Any difficulty once identified needs to have strategies put in place to reduce the impact of the problem on learning.

Contents of this section:
- strategies to support pupils with over-/undersensitivity of touch, light and sound;
- possible visual difficulties and suggested strategies to support development;
- additional classroom strategies to support vision;
- possible auditory difficulties and strategies to support development;
- promoting attention control and listening skills.

Supporting pupils with over/under-sensitivity to touch, light and sound

Pupils may have:

oversensitivity to noise/light/touch; the pupil:

- does not like different textures, e.g. eating, touching;
- does not like to get his/her hands sticky;
- is intolerant of loud noises, e.g. clapping in assemblies;
- avoids touching objects/peers;
- avoids rough-and-tumble play.

undersensitivity to noise/light/touch; the pupil:

- is always touching things;
- seeks vestibular stimulation, e.g. spinning, roundabouts, flings him/herself around;
- likes and seeks noise/stimulus, etc.;
- generally crashes around bumping into objects and people;
- really enjoys rough play.

Strategies to support the pupil:

- sit the pupil in a quiet area with minimal visual stimulus;
- do not force him/her to take part in an activity that he/she does not feel comfortable with;
- discuss different aspects of touch, e.g. things that are dry/sticky/rough/smooth, etc.;
- ditto with taste;
- try to develop touch by having different textured resources, e.g. a variety of balls/beanbags in PE, feely bags, etc.;
- give him/her activities using clay or plasticine which require more strenuous pressure;
- allow the pupil to sit near the door in assemblies or wear ear plugs;
- structure playtimes and encourage the pupil to take part in different activities.

Strategies to support the pupil:

- sit the pupil in the least busy part of the classroom to reduce stimulus;
- give the pupil something to play with, e.g. Blu-tack to keep hands busy;
- have a quiet area with no visual stimulus for time out/story;
- have quiet music playing in the background to promote a calm environment;
- begin morning and afternoon sessions with 2–3 minutes of stillness, e.g. 'hook ups' from Brain Gym, breathing in and out to a count of 5 or 6, visualisation, etc.;
- discuss 'personal space' and include in role play;
- pretend to be a mouse/elephant: 'How would you stroke these?' etc.;
- structure playtimes to limit the opportunities for rough play.

If the pupil does not improve, seek further advice from either a paediatric occupational therapist or the school's educational psychologist.

Visual perception difficulties and strategies to support development

Some pupils with co-ordination difficulties may experience problems wth visual perception

Problem with:	Examples:	Strategies to support development:
Visual tracking	• tracking a ball through the air; • eyes jumping over letters/words/lines when reading, writing or copying work; • setting out maths work (reversing/transposing symbols).	• use balloons/soft balls/bean bags, etc. (less threatening). • tracking exercises, e.g. from Brain Gym; • use a 'Reading Helper' (see Resources); • to support copying from the board use different pens on each line or quarter the board. • provide maths templates (page 117); • 'Roll 'n' Write Numbers' from LDA. NB: Pupils may need to be referred to an optician.
Visual spatial relationships	• bumping into objects/ furniture; • judging distances; • judging positioning of objects	• feel or count corners of cubes/ tables/chairs, etc.; • provide brightly coloured furniture. • draw a metre grid on the hall floor – place a beanbag in one square and ask the pupil to judge how far away it is; • ask the pupil how far he/she needs to move to reach the beanbag; • use the Roamer. • provide large-size toys/pencils/paint-brushes to start with; • encourage the pupil to hold objects in the midline with both hands.
Figure/ground discrimination	• finding a toy/object on a patterned carpet; • finding his/her work drawer/coat peg/ books, etc.; • identifying a ball thrown to him/her;	• use brightly coloured toys; • ensure that there is a plain carpet in play areas. • colour-code coat pegs/work drawers/books, etc.; • use large brightly coloured balloons/ balls, etc.; • give the instruction 'Watch for the red/blue balloon/ball and get ready to catch it...'

	• identifying a car approaching on the road;	• incorporate into road safety – ask pupils to listen for traffic and watch for a red/blue car approaching, etc.;
		• ask them to count slowly once they can see the car – the time should increase as they become more aware of traffic.
	• locating furniture in a busy classroom;	• simplify the classroom layout leaving space around furniture for movement;
		• use brightly coloured furniture;
		• mark the edges of table with brightly coloured tape.
	• making sense of pictures;	• use inset boards, mosaics, jigsaws;
		• recognise an object while slowly revealing it.
	• understanding picture sequences to make a story;	• use simple black and white lined pictures;
		• talk about what is in the picture with the pupil;
		• ask the pupil to colour in the main object/person in the picture.
	• finding charts/maps difficult to read;	• produce large, simple, uncluttered charts;
		• enlarge maps and colour-code;
		• provide a perspex grid to put over maps to help the pupil orientate him-/ herself.
	• finding that words merge together on the page.	• use a ruler or 'Reading Helper' to isolate the line; point to, or use two L- shaped pieces of card to isolate words;
		• request that the pupil is tested for scotopic sensitivity.
Form/size constancy	• recognising that an object seen close up is the same when seen in the distance, or from another angle;	• match different sized pairs (objects/ pictures);
		• give the pupil three different objects and ask him/her to match to one three metres away, increase distance and similarity/number of objects gradually;
		• ask the pupil to match a picture on the desk to one stuck on the wall;
		• match pictures of objects taken from different perspectives.
	• recognising that a word is the same regardless of size or font.	• provide sets of words in different fonts/ sizes/colour, etc. and ask them to match a given word;
		• cut out the word shape and ask them to match it to the correct word.

Maintaining eye contact (some pupils find maintaining eye contact threatening)	• making either too long or too short eye contact (resulting in problems with social interaction).	• request pupils to 'Look at me' when giving instructions to the class; • use puppets to encourage eye contact (less threatening); • discuss eye contact and its part in social interaction, e.g. paying attention, consideration, smiling, making friends; • use 'Socially Speaking', or computer programs (e.g. 'Smart Alex') to develop social interaction skills.
Visual closure	• deducing information from incomplete visual diagrams/pictures.	• identify a shape from part of the shape; • slowly reveal pictures; • complete a partially drawn shape/ object.

Additionally, for writing spatial concepts are involved:

Spatial awareness/ orientation Check: does the pupil understand positional words, e.g. beside/next to/right/ left?	• overlapping letters or written on top of the previous letter;	• use 'Write from the Start' to develop visuo-spatial skills; • have pupils stand beside/next to one another in PE; • give each pupil in the class a letter and spell out short words in the left to right order – draw a grid on the floor in which he/she can stand to reinforce spacing.
	• spacing between words missing;	• use finger/card spacer;
	• letters reversed or upside down, mirror writing, etc.	• check for cross-laterality (eye–hand dominance – page 56), which may cause problems with left/right orientation, reversals, etc.; • use a multi-sensory approach, touch and sight using three-dimensional letters, or LDA 'Roll 'n' Write' letters; • give visual perception exercises, e.g. ring all the letter 'b's; • have one pupil write a letter on the back of another, who should guess what it is; • use 'word play' prompts, e.g. bat and ball for the letter 'b'.
Spatial relationships (understanding how two or more objects relate to one another)	• spelling and reading problems – also linked to visual memory and visual sequential memory.	• use spelling games; • use simple mnemonics to aid spelling, e.g. bat and ball for 'b'.

Additional classroom strategies to support visual perception

For those pupils who have problems with visual perception there are a variety of ways in which the teacher can support them in the classroom:

- Reduce visual clutter in displays to avoid visual overload and ensure that information progresses from left to right.
- Provide simple, clear worksheets and activity cards.
- Enlarge text and use double spacing. If possible, use the Sassoon Primary Infant Font (created for visual clarity for use with primary-aged pupils).
- Seating position in the class is important. The pupil should sit facing the blackboard and teacher, not at an angle to it, since this distorts visual perception, for all copying work.
- Provide a fixed-angled board for copying work (see Sitting position for classroom activities) since this reduces the range of eye movement required between model and reproduction.
- Allow the pupil to write on alternate lines, which reduces visual clutter.
- Encourage the pupil to hold the reading book upright when reading since this reduces visual distortion of text.
- Use a multi-sensory approach to pre-writing skills (see Fine motor skills), to teach individual letter shapes and spellings.
- Teaching cursive script rather than print means that the hand learns the 'shape' of the whole word, which helps with spellings. NB: Refer to the school's policy on handwriting for guidance regarding this.

Auditory difficulties and strategies to support development

Problem with:	Examples:	Strategies to support development:
Auditory discrimination	• recognising everyday sounds; • identifying the same letter sound when at the beginning/middle/end of a word.	• match picture to sound on tape; • 'Simon Says…'/'I spy…', etc.; • Chinese whispers. • sound matching – say a sound and ask the pupil to put up his/her hand when he/she hears the sound again. • 'I Spy' with initial/end letter sounds plus vowel; • refer to SENSS for more specific intervention.
Rhythm	• recognising and copying.	• join in nursery rhymes/songs; • play marching songs in different tempos in PE; • copy a tapped pattern; • tap out the syllables in names/words, etc. on a drum.
Auditory selection (pupils may switch off and appear to daydream if there is a problem in this area)	• being able to pick out sounds/instructions, etc. from a busy background; • picking out the sound of a car from street sounds.	• use a small bell to signal that pupils listen for a new instruction; • ask the pupil to clap when he/she hears a certain voice on a tape. • see figure/ground discrimination on page 34.
Auditory memory	• remembering instructions.	• Chinese whispers; • shopping games – 'I went to the Shops and I Bought an Apple…', each pupil adds something; • each child adds a word to a sentence, etc.
Control of pitch	• being able to moderate voice appropriately, i.e. speak softly/loudly.	• whispering games; • 'How do you speak to the person next to you/across the classroom?', etc.; • act out stories with contrasting characters, e.g. Jack and the Beanstalk, Goldilocks, etc.; • use puppets if pupils lack confidence.

Gross motor skills

Motor control is gained from the head downwards to the feet and from the midline of the body out to the fingers.

Additionally, the left side of the brain controls the right side of the body and vice versa. This effectively results in an invisible midline running down the length of the body and young children must learn to work *around* this midline. The pupil must also learn to co-ordinate both sides of the body if he/she is to walk, run or kick a ball while balancing on the other leg, etc.

Contents of this section:

- The following pages provide an overview of gross motor skills progression.
- Staff will be able to judge approximate skill level through observation of the pupil in playground activities and PE sessions.
- Discussion with parents will also provide relevant information, e.g. delayed physical milestones, crawling stage missed out, etc. The latter has implications for bilateral co-ordination and both body and spatial awareness.
- Pages 42–6 provide a tick list to give a baseline regardless of whether the pupil has a physical delay only, or if the delay is global.

The activities on the right of these pages may be included in PE/play to develop the skill objective. Try to put them into a play/game context if possible, e.g. when 'long sitting' (sitting on the floor with back against the wall and legs straight out) to develop sitting balance, sit a number of pupils 30cm apart in a line and play 'Pass the Hot Potato'. This also combines cross-body movements.

Subsequent pages provide:

- points to bear in mind when setting up a small-group activity session for pupils with co-ordination difficulties;
- guidance for extending skills in the Early Years;
- ideas for promoting physical skills with secondary-aged pupils.

Overview of gross motor skill progression

Staff need to be aware of the developmental sequence for the acquisition of gross motor skills and that they are built up hierarchically, i.e.:

→ core stability (head control, sitting balance, shoulder and hip fixation) underpins standing balance; leading to

→ bilateral integration (walking, balancing on one leg, hopping, running, jumping, climbing, skipping, etc.);

→ eye–hand–foot co-ordination for throwing, catching, kicking, etc.

3 months	• sits with back straight apart from lower lumber region; • on tummy, lifts head and upper chest using forearms to support; • on back kicks legs alternately.
6 months	• lying on back raises head; • sits with support; • if hands are held, braces shoulders and pulls to sitting; • on tummy, lifts head and upper body on flat hands and straight arms; • when held, takes weight on feet and bounces up and down.
9 months	• sits on floor unaided for 10–15 minutes; • leans forward, turns to look sideways, stretches out to pick up a toy; • progresses along the floor by rolling; • pulls to standing holding onto furniture; • attempts to crawl; • held upright, steps with alternate feet.
12 months	• sits on floor for indefinite time; • can rise to sitting from lying down; • pulls to standing and down again holding onto furniture; • walks around furniture side-stepping; • may stand alone; • walks forward with hand held.
15 months	• kneels unaided or with minimum support on floor; • can get to feet and down again without holding on; • creeps upstairs safely; • walks alone with uneven steps, arms held fixed or out to aid balance.
18 months	• kneels upright on flat surface without support; • flexes knees and hips to pick up toy from the floor, using hands to help, then rises to feet alone; • walks independently, stopping and starting safely; • runs carefully in straight line, looking at ground, head in the midline.
2 years	• squats safely to play; • sits on small tricycle and propels with feet on the floor;

	• can stop/start/turn around safely; • climbs on furniture and can get down safely; • walks up and down and sometimes downstairs holding rail safely; • walks into a large ball to try to kick it; • throws a small ball overhand.
2½ years	• jumps with both feet together from a low step; • can stand on tiptoe when shown; • walks upstairs confidently holding rail; • walks downstairs two feet to a step; • runs, and climbs on nursery equipment safely; • throws ball at body level; • kicks a large ball gently.
3 years	• sits with feet crossed at ankles; • stands on tiptoe; • stands on preferred foot briefly; • jumps when shown from bottom step of stairs safely; • walks forwards/backwards/sideways with confidence; • rides a tricycle using pedals; • runs around obstacles safely; • throws a ball overhand; • catches large ball on, or between, extended arms; • kicks a large ball forcibly.
4 years	• picks up objects from the floor by bending from the waist with knees extended; • sits with knees crossed; • stands on preferred foot for 3–5 seconds; • hops on preferred foot; • walks up- and downstairs one foot to a step; • walks and runs on tiptoe; • climbs ladders/trees; • increasingly skilful at throwing/catching/bouncing/kicking balls.
5 years	• stands on either foot for 8–10 seconds on preferred foot with arms folded; • walks along a narrow line; • skips on alternate feet; • hops 2–3 metres on either foot; • skilful at climbing/sliding/swinging, etc.

It is important to remember that:

• a child cannot perform a skill out of sequence;

• problems frequently arise from low muscle tone, which results in slower progress of the acquisition of skills.

Reference

Overview of gross motor skills adapted from Sheridan, M. (2003) *From Birth to Five Years*, Routledge.

Gross motor skill checklist and activities

Skill area to be checked:	If not, try the following activities:
Rolling – can the pupil: ❑ travel along a mat by rolling	– roll on stomach/back on request; – roll downhill on a wedge shape; – play 'There Were Ten in a Bed…'
Sitting balance – can the pupil: ❑ sit on a chair maintaining a good upright position for working	– long sitting; – sitting cross-legged on the floor, play 'I'm a Little Teapot'; – free sit on the floor with arms out straight at the side, rock from side to side (aeroplanes, turn right/left, etc.); – sit and balance on a wobble board.
Crawling – can the pupil: ❑ crawl forwards/backwards/over/under/around, etc.	– move forwards/backwards using arms only, lying on a scooter board; – in the crawl position raise left/right arm alternately; – in the crawl position raise left/right leg alternately; – Superman/woman raising opposite arm and leg; – 'Cats and Camels', i.e. hump and hollow back in the crawl position; – crawl over obstacles of varying heights and textures; – crawl around a circuit, e.g. shipwreck (dry land and water).
❑ crawl through a tunnel	– crawl through a hoop/line of hoops; – crawl through a small tunnel made of PE equipment; – crawl through partially extended tunnel.
❑ crawl along a bench	– crawl along a line; – crawl along/around the edge of a PE mat; – crawl over a line of thick cushions.

Kneeling – can the pupil:	
❏ maintain a kneeling position for 5 minutes	– let the pupil high kneel with arms on the table; – work at the table in a high kneeling position; – from a crawl position, sit back on his/her heels.
❏ walk in a high kneeling position	– paint at an easel in a high kneeling position; – kneel on one leg and raise the other leg at right angles, hold arms out at the side; – same position, fold arms and balance; – work at the table in a high kneeling position; – move around the table, to next activity, in high kneeling position.
Balance in walking – can the pupil:	
❏ 'stop' on request when walking, e.g. 'Statues'	– play 'Statues', traffic light game, 'What Time Is It, Mr Wolf?' etc.
❏ walk along a straight line marked on the floor	– walk between tramlines on the floor, gradually reducing distance between lines; – walk along a wide ribbon.
❏ walk on tiptoes, heels, etc.	– rock forwards on toes; – swing arms and reach as high as you can; – reach high and lean forwards, staying on toes; – sit on chair and raise toes; try to rise in this position; – lean against the wall and raise toes.
❏ step over an obstacle	– step over a beanbag on the floor; – step over a cane on the floor, gradually raise it higher off the floor.
❏ walk along a low bench	– walk between tramlines on a PE mat; – walk over a line of cushions on the floor.
❏ walk in and out of objects	– walk around one object and back (relay races); – walk between two obstacles; – increase number of obstacles and weave between (relay races).
❏ follow cutout footprints on the floor	– step over canes evenly spaced; – walk one foot to a square grid, gradually reduce in size.

❏ balance a beanbag on the back of one hand	– walk with large ball held in both hands; – walk with beanbag held in both hands; – walk with beanbag resting on upturned hand;
❏ balance a beanbag on his/ her head	– walk with large hat on his/her head, then smaller hat; – walk with a quoit on his/her head.
Balancing on one leg – can the pupil: ❏ march, getting knees as high as possible	– walk on the spot, gradually raising knees higher; – doing this to music will help establish a rhythm, begin with fast music then slow down rhythm.
❏ walk sideways	– single sideways step, both ways, increase number of steps (e.g. a simple line-dancing routine).
❏ follow well-spaced 'stepping stones' making giant steps, walking slowly	– step over a series of beanbags in a line; – stride from one mat to another across a gap, increase gap; – walk, placing one foot to each hoop set in a line, increase gap.
Climbing – can the pupil: ❏ climb up wall bars (be aware that some children may have problems with depth perception as well as poor co-ordination skills)	– climb in and out of a box; – crawl through a tunnel; – step over/on/off graded obstacles, steps, etc.; – climb stairs one at a time.
Running – can the pupil: ❏ run safely on tiptoes	– walk heel to toe along a line; – stand on tiptoe and turn around; – walk on tiptoe, increase speed.
❏ run around obstacles changing direction easily	– walk, weaving in and out of a cone slalom course; – move alternate cones out to each side making direction changes more acute; – obstacle team races, walk slowly first, then faster.
Jumping – can the pupil: ❏ jump off the bottom step holding hands	– bend knees and reach up high quickly; – run and jump over beanbag, etc.

❑ jump on the spot	– infant trampoline; – step on and off a kerb; – play 'Jack in a Box'.

Throwing – can the pupil:
❑ throw a large ball at a target
    (NB: Use a range of balls with
    different textures and sizes)
	– roll a ball to partner using both hands;
	– roll a ball around his/her feet and back;
	– push a ball at a large target on the wall;
	– sit on a bench and push a large ball off
	  his/her knees towards the wall target;
	– stand and drop the ball into a hoop,
	  increase the distance gradually.

❑ throw a ball underarm with
    preferred hand to a partner
	– throw a beanbag into a hoop, increase the
	  distance;
	– throw a beanbag at a target on the wall;
	– try using different types of ball to hit the
	  target.

❑ throw a ball overarm with
    preferred hand
	– throw a beanbag as hard as possible at
	  the floor;
	– throw a beanbag into a large container on
	  the floor;
	– throw a beanbag at a target on the wall,
	  start close to and increase distance.

Catching – can the pupil:
❑ catch a large ball
	– play 'Pass the Ball' over his/her head with
	  both hands to a partner;
	– roll a ball around his/her body;
	– roll and stop a ball in a group circle;
	– roll a ball along a table top and stop it at
	  the other end;
	– throw up and catch a balloon or a large
	  soft ball (these move more slowly);
	– drop a large ball with two hands and
	  catch, increase force used;
	– bounce a large ball to a partner for
	  him/her to return.

Kicking – can the pupil:
❑ kick a large ball while standing
	– kick a ball when seated on a high chair;
	– hold on between two chairs and kick a
	  large ball;
	– hold one chair (same side as dominant
	  foot) and kick the ball.

❏ run at a ball and kick it	– walk into a balloon/large soft ball and kick it without intent; – run at a balloon/large soft ball and kick it.
❏ dribble a ball	– walk and gently kick a balloon/large soft ball, follow it and kick again; – walk and dribble a balloon/large soft ball around a short slalom course.
Hopping and skipping – can the pupil: ❏ hop forwards three metres	– hold the pupil's hands and ask him/her to jump, encourage him/her to try to use one leg only; – hop holding onto a chair back; – hop around a table holding on.
❏ skip in a straight line	– hop on the spot and change feet after two hops; – hop and change feet after one hop; – hop to a rhythm around the room.
Midline awareness and bilateral integration – can the pupil: ❏ cross the midline of the body	(to ensure ability to co-ordinate both limbs by crossing the midline of the body) – cross-crawling; – touch right elbow to left knee, etc. standing up (Brain Gym activities, etc.); – do the 'Hokey-Cokey'; – bend foot up backwards and touch foot with the opposite hand behind his/her back; – PE activities such as ribbon work, team games (e.g. pass the beanbag standing sideways); – copying actions, 'Simon Says', etc.

Small-group activity work

Some pupils benefit from a more structured approach to address physical difficulties, especially if confidence is low and they are reluctant to participate in group activities.

When planning a programme for small-group work, either select one activity from each skill area and vary the programme as skills progress, or concentrate on one area as a 'theme'.

Example of group session – focus on running balance

1. Warm-up exercises:
   a. shaking hands, arms, one leg and then the other, whole body;
   b. swing arms to cross in front of the body and then swing them up high (windmills);
   c. stretching up tall onto toes, stretching arms and legs as wide as possible.
2. Walking race in which each pupil must walk heel to toe along a line.
3. Ditto walking on hands and toes.
4. Run around the room on tiptoes.
5. Running race, there and back, around a cone at the far side of the hall.
6. Individual timed activity running around a slalom course of cones; increase the number of cones as ability improves.
7. Wind down activity, e.g.:
   a. shake arms while jogging on the spot;
   b. reach up high and stretch up tall on tiptoes, slowly bring arms down;
   c. lie down and breathe quietly for 1 minute.

- Pupils often have spatial problems so limit the amount of equipment per session.
- Encourage pupils to work within a defined space, e.g. chalk a grid, or place carpet squares, on the hall floor and instruct them to work within the square. A chalk grid could be numbered so the pupil knows which the 'home' square is and then move as directed by the teacher, e.g. take two steps sideways, back one, etc.
- Always have a warm-up period, revisit previous skills learned, introduce new skills and finish with a quiet reflective wind-down prior to going back to class.
- Teach new skills in small stages if necessary; this will help to build up control.
- To demonstrate improvement to the pupil, keep a record of progress. NB: The pupil is always competing with him-/herself, not with others.

Early Years pupils:

- If the pupil has difficulties riding a tricycle, work on these checklist activities:
  - balancing on one leg/hopping to build up upper trunk balance;
  - climbing, to build up leg muscle strength.
- Pupils with poor balance will be afraid to go on the climbing frame. Grade climbing activities, e.g. have boxes of different sizes to climb in and out of; instruct pupils to climb *around* the frame rather than *up*.

- To develop spatial awareness further get the pupils to work within a hoop, e.g. be a statue, march/run/jump/hop on the spot, climb through, walk around the outside clockwise/anticlockwise, etc.
- With a pupil showing overflow of movement to upper limbs, e.g. arms moving like windmills when running, instruct to keep elbows bent and tucked in to the side.
- For those whose arms flap when asked to balance on one leg, instruct to keep arms straight down by the side of the body like a soldier.
- If this does not work, give the pupil water-filled milk cartons to carry to weigh down his/her arms; gradually reduce the amount of water, etc.
- Always involve parents so that they can follow the same method. A united approach reduces confusion and helps the pupils to learn a skill more quickly.
- Encourage parents to take the pupil swimming, play football with mum/dad or siblings, go to the adventure playground in the park, ball pools attached to supermarkets/stores, etc. (see parental handout 1 on page 118).

Secondary-aged pupils

- Watch for any strengths in PE and encourage the pupil to stretch him-/herself in that particular area.
- Encourage the pupil to work on developing muscle strength, e.g. weight training if the school has a multi-gym, etc. NB: If the pupil is under the supervision of a paediatric physiotherapist or occupational therapist, discuss what would be most appropriate before beginning any programme.
- If no multi-gym is available, devise a fitness programme, e.g.:
    - upper body weight bearing activities, e.g. press-ups, handstands against the wall, balancing activities on the horse/box;
    - endurance activities, e.g. running, football, tennis, etc.

    These improve both motor skills and all-round self-confidence.
- Always try to work with a small group rather than individually since this reassures the pupil that 'others have problems too'.
- Aim for a minimum of three short sessions a week rather than a longer single session.
- Encourage out-of-school activities which help to develop hand–eye co-ordination and confidence, e.g. tennis, golf, judo, etc.

Fine motor skills

In this section page 50 provides an overview of fine motor skill progression. Approximate ages are given as a guide to the 'normal' stages of development.

There are five areas of skill development referred to in this section:

 grasp;

 hand dominance;

 mark making;

 bilateral integration;

 hand–eye co-ordination.

- Skills are organised into a hierarchical order and a key is used for clarification.
- A checklist with suggested activities to develop each skill area is included on page 52.

The checklist on page 52 can be used to record achievement and may also be used to identify weaknesses in a specific area of skill development. The skill focus and examples of activities to address weaknesses are again arranged in a hierarchical order.

- In many cases these activities will already be part of good classroom practice.
- There is inevitably some repetition in the suggested activities as many activities will address more than one skill area.
- Children who present difficulties within this area may have an uneven profile with gaps in skill development.
- When working with older pupils, careful planning will be required to ensure that activities are modified to provide age-appropriate interventions.

Overview of fine motor skill progression

🖐 Grasp   Bilateral integration

🖐 Hand dominance   ◆ Hand–eye co-ordination

✏ Mark making

6 months	🖐	holds toys in a palmar grasp (whole hand) and passes from hand to hand;
	🖐	picks up objects by scooping with both hands.
9 months	🖐	isolates index finger to poke at a small object;
	🖐	begins to use pincer grasp (index finger and thumb).
12 months	🖐	picks up small objects using fine pincer grasp between tip of index finger and thumb;
	🖐	begins to show hand dominance.
15 months	🖐	uses pincer grasp with both hands at the same time;
	✏	scribbles backwards and forwards using a palmar grasp in either hand;
		&
	◆	builds a tower with 2 cubes following a demonstration.
18 months	🖐	shows signs of developing a crude thumb and 2-finger grasp;
	🖐	picks up small objects accurately;
	🖐	turns pages several at a time;
	🖐	points with precision at pictures in a book;
	🖐	most children will now have a hand dominance;
	✏	scribbles and makes dots;
		&
	◆	builds a tower of 3 cubes following demonstration (sometimes spontaneously).
2 years	🖐	good manipulative skills, now picks up and places objects neatly and with accuracy;
	🖐	turns single pages in a book;
	✏	holds a pencil using thumb and first 2 fingers;
	✏	draws spontaneous circular scribble and dots;
	✏	imitates vertical lines and sometimes V-shapes;
	◆	builds a tower with 6 or 7 cubes.

2½ years		holds a pencil in an improved tripod grasp;
		has a dominant hand;
		imitates a horizontal line, a circle;
		imitates 'T' and 'V';
		builds a tower of 7+ bricks using dominant hand.
3 years		picks up very small objects using pincer grasp;
		can close fist and wiggle thumbs of both hands in imitation;
		can hold pencil in dominant hand with 2 fingers and thumb;
		draws horizontal and vertical lines;
		copies 'O V H T';
		imitates 'X';
		draws a person with a head and 2 more parts or features;
		builds a bridge using 3 bricks after a demonstration.
4 years		copies 'X';
		draws 'O V H T';
		draws a person with head, trunk, legs, and usually arms and fingers;
		draws a recognisable house;
		&
		threads small beads;
		builds towers of 10+ cubes;
		builds bridges spontaneously using 3 bricks.
5 years		counts fingers of one hand using index finger of other;
		copies squares;
		copies triangles (by 5½);
		writes a few letters spontaneously;
		copies 'V T H O X L A C U Y';
		draws a person with head, trunk, legs, arms, fingers and features;
		draws a house with windows, doors, roof and chimney;
		draws pictures with several items and shows an indication of background;
		colours pictures staying mainly within the lines;
		&
		threads a large needle;
		builds 3 steps using 6 cubes following a demonstration.

Reference
Overview of fine motor skills adapted from Sheridan, M. (2003) *From Birth to Five Years*, Routledge.

Fine motor skill checklist and activities

Skill area to be checked:	If not, try the following activities:
Grasp – can the pupil: ❑ hold objects in a palmar grasp (whole hand)	– provide a wide range of toys to stimulate interest; encourage the child to reach out and grasp with both hands; – pick up and release a foam ball; – pick up and pass small ball from hand to hand.
❑ use index finger in isolation (pointing)	– teach finger rhymes such as 'Two Little Dickie Birds'; – use finger puppets on the index finger; – press keys of a toy telephone, till, toy musical instruments; – encourage finger painting; – encourage recorder playing/piano/keyboard playing; – teach keyboard/typing skills.
❑ hold objects in pincer grasp (index finger and thumb)	– pop bubble wrap between finger and thumb; – peg out washing (or paintings) to dry; – inset jigsaws (reducing in size); – bulldog clips to fasten paper; – sorting activities using small objects.
❑ hold a pencil in tripod grasp	– use activities above to develop a tripod grip; – try a range of pencil grips.
Other considerations ❑ use finger and thumb in opposition	– touch each finger in turn using the thumb; – pick up small toys using tweezers or tongs; – roll plasticine or playdough between finger and thumb; – play with 'popper-beads'; – play with wind-up clockwork toys; – fasten press-studs on clothing.

❏ demonstrate acceptable finger/hand strength	– squeeze playdough, stress balls; – playdough and plasticine activities; – tug of war; – water race where water is transferred from one container to another by filling and squeezing sponges; – hand jives/hand warm-up exercises; – squeezing citrus fruits on a traditional lemon squeezer; – chair press-ups; – write/draw with carbon paper under to encourage pressure; – offer squiggle pens and light pens, which give sensory feedback with sufficient pressure; – use of a paper punch and stapler.
❏ rotate wrists/forearm	– nut and bolt toys; – wring out cloths and dolls' clothes; – look through a kaleidoscope; – sharpen pencils.
Hand dominance – can the pupil: ❏ demonstrate hand dominance 	– encourage two-handed scribbling; – observe pupil at play and present work from the side he/she favours more for using a phone, telescope and kicking a ball; – place a small whiteboard end on to the pupil and get the pupil to draw patterns on both sides at same time (after a week the stronger side will usually appear).

Mark making – can the pupil:
Remember children learn to imitate first then copy.
Imitate = reproduce after a demonstration
Copy = reproduce from model
 	
❏ scribble to and fro holding pencil with palmar grasp
❏ scribble and make dots holding pencil in pincer grasp
❏ imitate vertical lines and sometimes V shapes
	Use a multi-sensory approach by selecting a range of activities taken from each of the sensory areas suggested below:
	
	– *gross motor movement:*
	  play with cars and push-along toys;
	– wipe the table with damp cloth;
	  swish hands in water and washing-up liquid to make bubbles;
	– make ribbon patterns in the air;

	– play marching games following the lines and direction of the desired pencil movement;
	– encourage visual tracking (following a moving object from left to right) with motorised remote control toys.
❏ imitate horizontal line	*visual stimuli:*
	– demonstrate movements in the air asking the pupil to imitate your actions;
❏ imitate a circle	– demonstrate mark making on white boards then ask the pupil to imitate your marks; when this is achieved move on to copying.
❏ imitate 'T' and 'V'	
❏ draw horizontal and vertical lines	*tactile (touch) stimuli:*
	– sand trays;
	– lentil, pasta trays;
	– playdough (see recipes);
	– finger paints (see recipes);
❏ copy 'O V H T'	– shaving foam;
	– 'Roll 'n' Write' cards;
❏ imitate 'X'	– use template to colour within a shape;
	– use glue pens to form a raised outline for colouring within.
❏ copy 'X O V H T'	
	olfactory (smell) stimuli (check that the selected medium is child-friendly; exercise caution with essential oils):
❏ copy squares	– use child-friendly scented crayons and markers;
	– use scented finger paints when providing tactile experiences;
❏ copy triangles	– experiment with fruit and vegetable printing to reinforce mark making and left to right tracking.
❏ write a few letters spontaneously	
	auditory (sound) stimuli:
	– use and reinforce directional language making sure the child understands when demonstrating up and down, forwards and backwards, over and under, left and right movements;
	– use 'listen and do'-type cassette tapes which reinforce listening skills and fine motor skills.

Drawing skills – can the pupil:	Backward chaining/small-step approach
	Break the task into a series of small steps. For example, when teaching how to draw a face:
❑ draw a person with head and two more features	– provide a series of drawings of faces with one feature missing;
❑ draw a person with head, trunk, legs and usually arms and fingers	– ask the child to identify the missing feature; – demonstrate completion of the picture.
❑ draw a person with head, trunk, legs, arms, fingers and features	– ask the child to complete the picture; – gradually increase the complexity of the task by removing prompts.
❑ draw a house with windows, doors, roof and chimney	
❑ draw a recognisable house	
❑ draw pictures with several items and show an indication of background	(The same model could be used for drawing a dog, cat, house.)
❑ colour pictures staying mainly within the lines	
Bilateral integration – (using two hands together sometimes, for different tasks) can the pupil:	
❑ hold an object in two hands and perform an action	– push a pram or a push-along toy; – hold steering wheel in toy car; – steer bike/trike by holding handle bars.
❑ use one hand to steady an object while playing	– insert jigsaws; – 'post' toys; – pretend and real baking (hold the bowl while stirring).
❑ hold an object in one hand while performing an action with the other	– peel a banana; – open a zip; – sharpen a pencil; – use a hairdryer and hairbrush together; – hold a cup while pouring water into it from a jug.

❑ pour a drink from a bottle into a cup without spilling	– pour and fill with marbles, pebbles, conkers, lentils, sand, water play.
❑ remove and replace a screw-top lid	– nut and bolt construction toys; – café bar in home corner.
Crossing the midline This is an important element of bi-manual integration (using two hands together). This can be encouraged using the following activities.	– dressing up games; – dressing toys; – sit cross-legged and pat opposite knee; – march and touch opposite knee; – cut food with knife and fork; – lazy eights (Brain Gym); – sort activities where objects have to be picked up with one hand and placed in a container at the other side.
Hand–eye co-ordination – can the pupil: ❑ build a tower with two cubes following a demonstration foam ❑ build a tower of three cubes following a demonstration (sometimes spontaneously) ❑ build a tower of six or seven cubes ❑ build a tower of more than seven bricks using the dominant hand ❑ build a bridge using three bricks after a demonstration ❑ build towers of more than ten cubes ❑ build bridges spontaneously using three bricks ❑ build three steps using six cubes following a demonstration ❑ thread a large needle ❑ thread small beads	– provide play opportunities with building blocks, starting with large lightweight blocks; – provide a range of construction toys including self-adhesive varieties (Velcro/magnetic/interlocking); – gradually reduce the size of blocks/cubes; – use modelling and demonstration techniques to encourage creativity; – group pupils of differing abilities to provide positive role models. – provide a range of threading activities starting with dowel rods and progressing to stiffened cord and laces; – provide a range of bodkins and needles so that the pupil can select equipment within his/her skill level thus ensuring success and reinforcing self-esteem.

Recipes for dough and finger paints

Sand Dough

2 cups sand
1 cup cornflour
1 1/2 cups hot water
2 tsp. alum (from chemists)

Mix sand, cornflour and alum, add
water and stir well. Cook over medium
heat stirring all the time.
NB: This dough will dry out.

Cornflour Finger Paint

Mix 2 cups of cornflour in a pan
and add water to make the consistency
of glue. Cook, stirring continuously
until it becomes a clear gel. Colour
with food colouring and cool.

Soap Flakes Finger Paint

Combine soap flakes with sufficient water
to make a 'gluggy' texture. Mix with an
electric beater to achieve a finger paint
consistency. Add food colouring.

Salt and Flour Finger Paint

1 cup flour
4 tsp. salt
7/8 cups cold water

Combine flour, salt and water. Add food
colouring or paint. Mix well and store in the
fridge.

Part 3

Strategies to address the educational implications of co-ordination difficulties

Classroom activities

This section offers advice and strategies on a range of topics related to developing recording skills. Much of the advice is based on existing good classroom practice, which can be observed in many mainstream schools.

The approaches suggested will benefit all pupils, not just those with co-ordination difficulties. Strategies are intended for use in the classroom but are also appropriate for use in small-group and individual settings.

Contents of this section:

- promoting a good sitting position for work;
- teaching handwriting;
- teaching cursive script;
- the procedure for assessing a pupil's writing;
- classroom intervention following assessment;
- alternative recording strategies;
- teaching keyboard skills;
- teaching dictation skills;
- teaching cutting skills.

Sitting position for class activities

A poor sitting position (below left) results in a lack of stability for working. Weight is not equally distributed and muscles in one area are more tense than in others.

The brain has to concentrate on maintaining a stable sitting position, which results in complex fine motor activities such as writing becoming more difficult.

A good sitting position (right) means sitting with:

- feet flat on the floor;
- bottom well back on the seat;
- back straight;
- head up and in the midline.

This provides a stable base and means that the hands can be used in bi-manual activities to the best effect.

Developing sitting balance in the Foundation Stage

To aid core stability and sitting balance provide opportunities for pupils to draw/paint in a variety of positions, e.g.:

- prone or lying on tummy;
- standing at an easel or using a chalkboard;
- high kneeling;
- side leaning (resting on one elbow);
- on all fours.

This allows them to experience pressure on different areas of the body and helps to develop proprioception (see page 4).

When writing, the pupil also needs good shoulder, forearm, wrist and hand stability.

- Develop shoulder and forearm stability by encouraging pupils to draw with their elbows resting on the table.
- If there is a problem with wrist and hand stability, provide an angled board (above) on which the pupil can rest his/her forearms. Ask the pupil to rest the little-finger side of the working hand on the surface.

The pupil (above right) is also sitting on a 'Movin' Sit' cushion, which tilts the pelvis forward resulting in a more upright position.

This might prove beneficial for pupils who always sit with a rounded back, often as a consequence of low muscle tone.

The board angle can be between 20 and 45 degrees depending on the pupil's needs.

A number are available commercially, such as 'Writestart Desk' from LDA or 'Write Angle' from Philip and Tacey. The pupil to the right is using a 'Posture Pack', made up of a rubber wedged cushion and a large rigid file, with a carry handle, into which the wedge fits. A large lever arch file is a cheaper option if only an angled writing board is required.

The last two options are more appropriate for the secondary setting, where pupils move from classroom to classroom throughout the day.

Remember to check that sitting position is correct when the pupil moves up through the school. In primary schools the size of furniture changes and pupils may be small or tall for their age. Therefore seating should be reviewed at least annually.

A rough guide to the correct height for table and chairs is:
- tables should be half the pupil's height;
- chairs should be a third of the pupil's.

Furniture of different sizes may be required in a classroom if there is a great difference in the height of pupils. This also applies if pupils are split up into ability groups for literacy and numeracy and move to different classrooms.

Adjustable height tables are available from a range of suppliers, e.g. Hope Education, Rompa, Vari-Tech Ltd, although they are fairly expensive. However, a few tables strategically placed in primary or in subject bases at secondary would fulfil most pupils' needs.

If it is not possible to provide lower tables and chairs, the pupil may require a foot block to support his/her feet to ensure stability (see left). For younger pupils a toilet step from Ikea/Mothercare may be appropriate, or there are a number of commercially available wooden stacking foot blocks which provide a choice of heights (5, 7.5 and 10 cm). This allows the correct height block to be used.

NB: If the pupil is under the supervision of a paediatric occupational therapist, always consult him/her if there are concerns about seating.

Teaching handwriting

Importance of correct letter formation

- Pre National Curriculum (NC) (DES 1989), most schools taught a printed script without exit strokes (ligatures). Schools developed their own handwriting styles and policies.
- Post NC a fluent cursive script has to be taught, but this is open to interpretation.
- The National Literacy Scheme requires the teaching of *"Automatic, legible, fluent, speedy and attractive handwriting by end of year 4..."* (DfEE 1998).
- It is important that the following are taught:
  - starting and finishing point;
  - flicks and tails;
  - clockwise and anticlockwise formation;
  - ascenders and descenders;

  if fluency is to be achieved.

NB: Be aware that children learn shapes in the following order:

- circle – 3 years;
- cross – 4 years 1 month;
- square – 4 years 6 months;
- triangle – 5 years 3 months.

Does your school policy on handwriting reflect this?

When the pupil can combine two letter elements he/she is ready to learn letter formation (see Progression of drawing skills in Appendix 3). Check readiness for writing by asking the pupil to copy the shapes on page 111 in Appendix 3.

Teaching handwriting in KS1

Developing good handwriting is dependent on the pupil sitting correctly, having stability of the upper torso, shoulder, forearm and wrist, and a secure pencil grasp (page 67) which allows flexibility in the hand and wrist. Then:

- Ensure that the pupil has plenty of experience of gross motor movements and a secure understanding of directional speech, e.g. up, round, down, across, stop, start, circle, left, right, forwards, backwards, clockwise, anticlockwise; this reinforces letter formation (this may be incorporated into PE lessons, e.g. team games, maypole/country dancing, using ribbon sticks).
- Alongside this give the pupil opportunities for multi-sensory work in forming basic letter shapes in sand, paint, lentils, etc. as outlined in Mark making (page 53).
- Teach numbers first since there are fewer numbers than letters.
- Teach letter families together, e.g. 'c a d g q and o' (all starting with an anticlockwise circle); 'r n m h b and p' (all beginning with a downstroke), 'k v w x and z' (all involving diagonals), etc.

- Write the letter on the board verbalising the movements as they are drawn, e.g. for the letter 'c': 'Imagine the face of a clock and start at one o'clock'; then moving anticlockwise: 'Curve down and round and end at five o'clock – now let's do it together…'
- Encourage pupils to draw the letter in the air using their whole arm and join in with the verbal directions as they perform the action.
- Transfer the movement to paper once it is fully understood; encourage the pupil to continue to verbalise the movements while forming the letter.
- Provide lined paper – instructing the pupil to sit the letter on the line.
- Additionally, two or three minutes of hand exercises just before starting to write, e.g. stretching, clapping, shaking, fingertip presses, prepares muscles and increases hand and wrist strength and flexibility.

Generally the school will have a handwriting policy, which will outline the way handwriting is to be taught: if flicks are taught right from the start, when script is introduced, whether lined paper is used, when writing with a pen is begun and what type of pen is used.

However, some pupils may need an individual approach which does not follow the school formula rigidly, e.g. for those pupils who have poorly formed writing, using a fine biro gives better results than using a gel ink or ink pen. Biros have a 'drag' on the page, whereas gel ink pens flow freely and run away for some pupils.

Teaching cursive script

Cursive handwriting is made up of a small group of rhythmic movements, i.e.:

- long and short strokes (as in 'b, d, f, i, k, l, t' above the line and 'p, q' below the line and many capitals);

- push and pull garlands (as in 'h, n, m, r, u, y');

- clockwise and anticlockwise loops (loops below the line as in 'g, y, f', and loops above the line as in 'e, f' and possibly others (depending on the school handwriting policy);

- clockwise ('b, p') and anticlockwise ('a, c, d, g, o, q') circles; to form a cursive 'c' ask the pupil to make waves, which sit on the line;

- zigzags ('k, q, w, v, z' and possibly 'y' depending on handwriting policy).

Pupils who have been taught to add 'flicks and tails' when printing letters should find these patterns relatively easy to copy. If necessary, allow pupils to practise forming them on the board using a whole-arm movement. NB: Up/down, etc. will have more relevance on a vertical surface and using the whole arm encourages the development of fluency.

These patterns will help to promote writing fluency. Many of these movements could also be included in PE, e.g. weaving through obstacles, or dance within a story setting. Performing these actions to music also establishes fluency of movement more easily.

Lined paper should be used with an intermediate line, if necessary, for writing practice. The teaching of 'flicks' should have established the connections between letters, but certain joins may need to be taught specifically since a number of pupils have real difficulties understanding where one letter starts and the next one begins, e.g.:

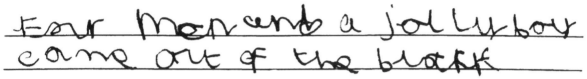

Aged 7 years

Note the 'ou' in the first word 'Four' (a clockwise 'o' and poorly joined 'ur'), in 'came' the 'm' has no initial downstroke, and the movements for the letters and joins required in the combinations for 'out' and 'ack', in 'black', are not understood at all (see page 74 for recommended intervention for this pupil).

Some schools teach cursive script right from the start, generally with great success. This establishes correct letter formation and the pupils learn to write only once. It also aids spelling since the hand learns the pattern of the word. However, opinions differ, therefore the decision to implement it or not must be left to the management team of individual schools.

Strategies to counter lack of improvement

If a multi-sensory approach to teaching handwriting is begun at the Foundation Stage and the child has moved through and achieved the hierarchical pre-writing skills of mark making, shape copying, combining letter elements and basic letter formation, writing should progress well. However, by KS1 and 2 problems may well be established.

Sometimes a highly structured programme of PE exercises, involving the development of hand–eye co-ordination, balance, spatial awareness and fine motor skill activities, e.g. accurate throwing and catching of balls/beanbags, may result in improved writing (rather than frequent repetition of practising, or redrafting, writing) – and is seen as 'fun'.

Performance improves for a number of reasons: increased skill level, raised self-esteem and confidence, better working relationships with staff and greater motivation to persevere.

Also assess handwriting using the forms provided in Appendix 4 and put intervention strategies in place, if appropriate.

Assessing handwriting

When assessing a sample of handwriting, observe how the pupil works, e.g.:

- Does the pupil have a good working posture?
- Is he/she tense, holds his/her breath, uses an unusual pencil grip?
- Check the position of the wrist – is it stiff and/or slightly hooked?

When observing the pupil writing, note:

- problems with formation of letters, e.g. clockwise 'o's;
- reversals (left to right or top to bottom);
- erratic sizing of letters;
- age-appropriate sizing, larger/smaller;
- alignment – does writing sit on the line/follow the margin?
- spacing – lack of/erratic;
- is writing laborious; does speed of production decrease after a short period?
- are mixed upper- and lower-case letters seen?
- is perseveration seen, e.g. not knowing when to stop when forming a circle?

For early writers use sample of handwriting sheets 1 and/or 2

Assess the pupil by asking him/her to:

- draw a picture of a person;
- write his/her name;
- copy or write the alphabet;
- copy or free write a short sentence.

For independent writers use sample of handwriting sheets 3 and/or 4

Assess the pupil by asking him/her to:

- copy the following sentence:

Four men and a jolly boy came out of the black and pink house quickly to see the bright violet sun but the sun was behind a cloud.

- also copy or free write to dictation:

the quick brown fox jumps over the lazy dog

Use the Assessment form on page 112 to record problems noted.

Intervention following assessment

The completed assessment form available, to go through point by point

The numbers below correspond to those on the assessment sheet. Numbers 1 to 5 are prerequisites and must be corrected before handwriting can be addressed.

1. Seating position for handwriting

The pupil should be in a good sitting position (see page 61), with feet flat and bottom to the back of the seat to provide a stable base and fix the trunk.

- Provide a fixed angled board or foot block to improve writing position, if required.
- Seat the pupil appropriately within the classroom (Classroom organisation – page 23).

2. Handedness

Left-handers need particular attention to ensure that they can both see their work and develop a suitable grip. Sit left-handers next to one another, or place them to the left of right-handers, to ensure that the writing arm is free.

3. Angling the paper

Angle the paper to the right or left depending on handedness – this reduces tension in the writing arm.

Left-handers should angle the paper to the right from 30 to 45 degrees as required. The paper should also be positioned slightly to the left of the body (see left).

For right-handers the paper should be angled 30 degrees to the left and positioned to the right of the body (see right).

4. Fixing

The pupil should hold the paper with his/her free hand to prevent the paper slipping. This helps to stabilise the trunk. For younger pupils use a visual prompt, e.g. stick an A4 piece of paper at the appropriate angle on the table top, with a cutout of the free hand superimposed on it.

For older pupils a line of coloured tape placed at the correct angle would be sufficient. If pupils are unable to fix the paper themselves, use Blu-tack, a rubberised non-slip mat or a clipboard.

5. Grasp

The standard tripod grip (right) is not always the most appropriate or comfortable for some pupils. As long as the grip is effective and relaxed, allow the pupil to continue using it.

It is generally possible to see if the grip is not effective, since the pencil will appear to be clenched in the hand.

Tension may also be seen in the wrist, which is rigid and sometimes slightly hooked, resulting in stiff, spiky writing, which is erratically sized, lacking in fluency.

Tense grips

If the pupil rolls his/her thumb over the index finger (left), the grip is generally tense and insecure.

Likewise, the pupil who holds his/her pencil along the barrel (right) will generally have difficulties gaining fluency.

The hooked wrist position is often used by left-handers since it allows them to see what is being written. When seen in right-handers, it is generally due to poor proprioceptive feedback (see page 4) from the wrist, elbow and shoulder. Both should be changed if possible. A weak grasp, which the pupil is constantly readjusting, should also be changed.

Changing a pencil grip

Often a moulded grip such as the 'Ultra' grip, which requires the pupil to position his/her fingers correctly, proves beneficial (see right).

This pencil grip is most suitable for primary-aged pupils.

Secure grips that can be tried are the four-fingered grip (similar to the tripod grip but using the ring finger as well) and the 'Monk's' grip (holding the pen between the index and middle fingers), illustrated left. Older pupils adapt to this grip well.

Additionally, have available a range of pencil grips as well as pencils with different-sized barrels (including maxi and triangular) for pupils to try.

For older pupils try the 'Tri-go' grip (left), the small 'Stubbi' or 'Stetro' grip (middle) and the 'Grip it' (right). The 'Handiwriter' (not shown) is a similar writing aid which attaches to the pencil above and below the thumb.

However, some older pupils may be too embarrassed to use a moulded grip. In this case use Blu-tack moulded to shape, or wrap one or two rubber bands around the barrel of the pencil at the usual holding position. Some pens now have integral rubber grips, which may prove sufficient.

Have available a range of pens for pupils to try. Include gel ink pens as well as ballpoints in the assessment kit, some with rubberised grips, since they each have a different 'feel' and what suits one pupil may not suit another.

Always ensure that the pen/pencil is not held too close to the end of the barrel since this can obscure work.

6. Too much or too little pressure

Training the proprioceptors (sensors in the joints) in the upper limbs will help, e.g.:

- ask the pupil to do 10 to 15 chair, or desk, 'press-ups' prior to writing activities;
- write on a paper sandwich with carbon paper between:
  - for pupils who apply too much pressure ask them *not* to mark the bottom paper (start with 3 sheets to allow them to observe gradual improvement);
  - for pupils who apply too little pressure, ask them to ensure that the carbon paper *is* marked;
- alternatively, raise the desk or provide an angled board for pupils whose pressure is too light on the paper and lower the desk for those who press too hard;
- prepare the muscles involved by doing 2–3 minutes of hand exercises before all writing activities, e.g.:
  - shake, flap or rotate hands;
  - 10 fingertip presses;
  - clench fists and release × 10;
  - walk fingertips along the desk;
  - touch thumb to each finger as quickly as possible;
  - finger rhymes such as 'Here's the Church, Here's the Steeple…';
- provide a softer pencil/fibre tip pen for pupils who apply light pressure.

7. Incorrect formation

- A pattern may be noted when looking at which letters were incorrectly formed by the pupil during the assessment, e.g. clockwise 'o's (which will impede the development of cursive script) used for 'a, g, o', etc.:
  - a gross motor programme concentrating on moving to speech directions would help the pupil to understand the difference between clockwise and anticlockwise;
  - also teach the movements required for that particular family of letters again (see page 64;
- The letters 'k' and 'x' involve diagonals and how they are formed will indicate whether the pupil has difficulties crossing the midline of the body (see pages 46 and 56);
- Also check if the pupil can copy flowing letter patterns.

8. Reversals

Often pupils with mixed laterality, i.e. right-handed but left-eye dominant, have problems with developing left/right orientation on the page, reversals of letters or words and mixing left/right sides of the body.

Check for cross-laterality and note down:
- which hand the pupil writes with;
- which foot he/she kicks with;
- which eye he/she uses to look through a telescope;
- which ear he/she uses to answer the phone.

For letter/number reversals, use a multi-sensory approach, e.g.:
- motor – draw the letter/number shape on the floor placing a green beanbag at the starting place and a red beanbag indicating where to stop; ask the pupil to walk around the shape while vocalising the movements;
- touch – write letter/number on the pupil's back and ask him/her to guess what it is;
- sight – use three-dimensional letters and ask the pupil to finger trace;
- auditory – encourage the pupil to verbalise the movements as he/she forms letters.

9. Erratic sizing

Use lined paper with additional guidelines for ascenders and descenders. Triple-lined paper, or books are available to purchase.

10. Alignment

If alignment is poor and work gradually wanders to the right of the page, use the traffic light system to aid setting out work, i.e.:

- put a green dot at the left side of the page to indicate 'start here';
- put a red dot at the right side of the page to indicate 'do not write beyond this spot';
- if necessary, put an orange dot 2 cm before the red dot to indicate 'do not begin a long word beyond this point'.

11. Spacing

To assist spacing, provide a paper, or card, word 'spacer'. The pupil may also use his/ her finger to separate words.

7., 9., 11., 12., 14. and 15.

These areas are most effectively addressed in the long term by using a structured perceptuo-motor programme, e.g. 'Write from the Start', which focuses on each skill area involved (Resources – page 129).

This is worked through as a whole for younger pupils. However, occasionally, older pupils' specific problems may be improved by working through two or three of the booklets – the Teacher's Manual lists the emphasis of each booklet.

NB: Be aware that some exercises are not age-appropriate for secondary pupils.

13. Fluency/speed

- Normal writing speed varies depending on the context, but progresses from an average of 1.5 words per minute at age five to 18 words per minute at sixteen (see sample of handwriting sheets 3 and 4 in Appendix 4).
- Writing speed should be checked before any intervention, then annually at least.
- To request special arrangements in exams the teacher must have up-to-date information regarding a pupil's speed of writing over a period of time.

Slant

It is now accepted that slant of writing should be given to individual preferences.

If a pupil is following a handwriting programme, do not insist on a similar slant to the model. It is correct formation that is the major concern in the development of a fluent script.

Assessment pack

Put together an assessment pack and have available:

- a selection of pencils, e.g. thin, chubby or triangular barrels, soft lead/hard lead, etc.;
- different pencil grips: triangular, soft foam, 'Ultra', 'Tri-go', 'Stretro' or 'Stubbi' moulded grips, 'Grip it', 'Handiwriter', etc.;
- a good selection of pens available for the pupil to try, e.g. pens with triangular or rubber grips, 'gel' or biro pens, etc. – generally available from good art shops;
- angled boards/large lever arch file (the cheap option to use as an angled board at secondary level)/Posture Pack, etc.;
- foot blocks of varying height (5, 7.5 and 10 cm) available to try if required;
- lined paper, including additional lines for guidance with ascenders and descenders;
- 'Speed Up' from LDA by Lois Addy (a book of exercises to help pupils build up fluency and writing speed).

See Resources and list of suppliers (page 129). Also look at spatial awareness/orientation on page 36. Use the 'keyboard skills' programme (page 78) to help the pupil develop the concept of 'spaces between words', since the use of the space bar is a deliberate action.

Handwriting samples

Sample 1

Aged 6 years

A pupil with significant fine motor co-ordination difficulties demonstrating the following:

- a weak two-fingered pencil grip;
- he could combine two letter elements (therefore ready to begin writing) and produce an approximation of his name;
- he was unable to draw a triangle (cross the midline);
- he was at a very early stage of writing.

Recommended intervention:

- to develop finger/hand strength – fingertip presses, popping bubble wrap, squeezing out sponges, making plasticine/clay models, etc.;
- provide an 'Ultra' pencil grip and work on developing a secure grasp;
- provide a fixed-angled board so the pupil can see work more easily (also improves pressure on paper);
- work on gross motor activities to reinforce letter formation and language of movement, e.g. letters on the floor in the hall (chalk or rope), the pupil walks around the shape describing movement; then teach letter families;
- to learn orientation of letters draw a letter on his back and ask him to guess what it is (develops orientation to his own body);
- work on crossing the midline (gross and fine motor);
- use 'Write from the Start' to develop perceptuo-motor skills;
- use alternative means of recording work to demonstrate ability;
- develop keyboard skills (to provide an alternative means of recording work).

Sample 2

Aged 7 years

A statemented pupil with a number of medical problems demonstrating the following:

- the pupil held the pencil with fingers arranged along the barrel therefore limiting control ('Ultra' grip provided);
- he could cross the midline but note problems with reversals ('s, z'); 'a, g, o, q' were produced using clockwise 'o's;
- erratic sizing of letters with 'p, g, q' standing on the line, mixed upper- and lower-case;
- copying flowing letter patterns – he began well, but could not sustain the fluid movement required due to a stiff, slightly hooked wrist.

Recommended intervention:

- work on gross motor movements for problem letters, i.e. where letters begin and end ('s, z', clockwise and anticlockwise letters);
- teach the 'o' letter family ('a, c, d, g, q, o') at the same time, followed by other letter families;
- follow a programme of activities to strengthen and improve flexibility in wrists, e.g. turning skipping rope, ribbon sticks, stir cakes at home;
- draw flowing letter patterns on the black-/whiteboard (as large as possible and ask him to reduce);
- to learn orientation of letters, draw a letter on his back and ask him to guess what it is (develops orientation to his own body);
- use 'Write from the Start' to develop perceptuo-motor skills;
- develop keyboard skills (to provide an alternative means of recording work).

Sample 3

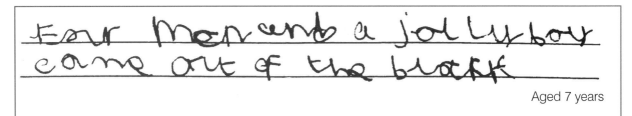

Aged 7 years

A Y3 pupil at School Action Plus of the CoP demonstrating the following:

- a secure four-fingered grip;
- he fixed with his free hand, but did not angle the paper;
- he could copy 2D shapes, but had problems with 3D shapes;
- he produced a cursive script, but did not understand the correct formation of some letters, e.g. 'o, a, d' (clockwise formation); however, note the 'o' in 'jolly' and 'boy' is correctly formed;
- he also had problems with 'd/b' (testing positive for cross-laterality);
- 'j, y' were above the line (no descenders);
- writing was erratic in sizing and spacing;
- his writing lacked fluency, but was age-appropriate for speed of production of work (28 letters per minute).

Recommended intervention:

- provide a template of writing position on his desk (indicating how much to angle the paper);
- strengthen hands and fingers, e.g. squeezing out sponges in the bath, helping Mum to wring out clothes, popping bubble wrap, etc.;
- draw flowing letter patterns on the black-/whiteboard (as large as possible to begin with and gradually reduce in size);
- draw lines of upper, middle and lower planes for guidance when practising ascenders and descenders – on the whiteboard first, then on paper;
- some parts of 'Write from the Start', i.e. dealing with fluency, sizing and spacing;
- draw letter on the pupil's back and ask him to guess what it is (develops orientation to his own body);
- teach keyboard skills (to provide an alternative means of recording work).

Sample 4

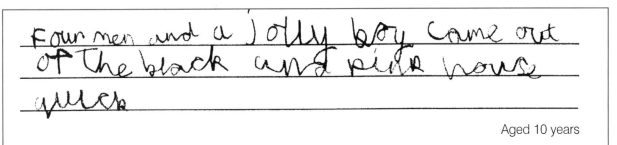

Four men and a jolly boy came out
of the black and pink house
quick

Aged 10 years

This pupil was being screened for dyslexia and was suspected of having scotopic sensitivity. He demonstrated the following:

- a secure tripod grip, did not angle the paper, but fixed with his free hand;
- he reported that he found white paper 'glaring';
- he tested positive for cross-laterality;
- he had no problem copying 2D and 3D shapes – could cross the midline and had a good awareness of spatial concepts;
- fluency of writing was developing (53 letters per minute, which is age-appropriate), but some erratic sizing was noted; however, spacing was good;
- formation was good apart from 'f, x';
- some descenders sat on the line, e.g. 'p, j'.

Recommended intervention:

- the provision of a line of tape on his desk (to show how to angle the paper);
- write on alternate lines to reduce visual clutter;
- use pastel-coloured paper (to reduce glare);
- staff should be aware of the possible problems associated with cross-laterality;
- he should work on some parts of 'Write from the Start', i.e. dealing with fluency;
- the provision of upper, middle and lower planes for guidance when practising ascenders and descenders – whiteboard first, then on paper;
- practice to improve formation of 'f, x' to enable him to form links correctly.

Sample 5

The quick brown fox jumps over the lazy dog!.

Aged 10 years

A Y6 pupil with a hemiplegia, very motivated and had worked very hard to develop a fluent cursive script. However, speed of work production decreased over time.

Sole recommendation:

- that the pupil develops touch typing skills and is lent a word processor to support recording work at secondary school.

Alternative recording strategies

Some pupils find recording in a conventional manner to be problematic and alternatives need to be considered.

Maths:

- The pupil solves the problem, points to the number on a number line and the adult writes the answer.

- Stickers with pre-written numbers are available for the pupil to peel off and stick onto his/her book, when he/she has completed the problem.

- Use number stamps to allow the pupil to put the answers onto his/her worksheet, book.

Written tasks:

- The younger pupil could produce a number of name labels on the computer, which he/she can stick onto paintings, etc. without having to struggle to write.

- The adult scribes at the pupil's dictation.

- The pupil records a sentence/story into a tape recorder and the adult transcribes.

- Cloze procedure, which can take a variety of forms:

  - sentences with a choice of words to circle, to allow the pupil to demonstrate his/her knowledge;

  - the pupil is given information prepared by the teacher, in a pictorial or written form; the pupil fills in gaps (in pictorial or word form) in order to demonstrate what knowledge he/she has acquired.

Goldilocks   **baby bear**

.... was in bed.

The pupil circles the word, copies the word or sticks a pre-written word in the space.

- Use Clicker 4 with key words programmed into a grid to support specific subject areas, e.g. history, geography. These can be purchased or downloaded.

- Use individual word banks with words attached with Velcro, which contain key words the pupil can read plus words linked to classroom work. The pupil composes the sentence, finds the words and attaches them to a Velcro strip. Matching words can then be available for the pupil to stick into his/her workbook if writing is difficult.

- Give multi-choice questions which allow the pupil to circle the correct answer.

- Provide opportunities for collaborative working where another pupil scribes the idea of the group.

- Use a word processor to allow the pupil to produce more attractive pieces of work, which can be illustrated using clip art, thereby overcoming poor drawing skills. It may be useful to teach touch typing skills for some pupils.

- Scanning of worksheets, etc. which can be adapted would allow the pupil to fill in the gaps to demonstrate levels of knowledge.

- Consideration should be given as to how pupils with poor recording skills make notes which they need to read back for revision. It may be possible for Dictaphones to be used, teacher notes to be made accessible or photocopying of a peer's notes to be allowed.

- It may be useful to teach dictation skills for some pupils (see page 83).

Teaching keyboard skills

Pupils with delayed writing skills should have access to a word processor or computer; this provides an alternative to handwriting, requiring minimal physical input, and provides an opportunity to produce work that looks age-appropriate.

Most pupils use the 'hunt and peck' method when typing. However, if keyboard skills are to be an effective alternative to writing, they need to be taught in a structured way, building up skills hierarchically. There are a number of pre-skills required:

- the pupil must have good sitting balance in order to use hands together;
- he/she must be able to isolate fingers (at least the index finger) on both hands.

If the pupil has effective use of one limb only, he/she must be able to stabilise the trunk with the weaker limb and isolate the index finger of the dominant hand.

With younger pupils, teaching the ability to write their names is motivating and teaches the placement of between 10 and 15 letters on the keyboard, as well as the function keys, space, return and backspace (delete). For example, if the pupil is called Robert, the first letter is pointed out on the keyboard with the instruction to press the 'r' and then space bar, to make a block of letters:

r r r r r r r r r r r r r r r r r r r
r r r r r r r r r r r r r r r r r r r

The pupil does not need to understand the difference between capitals and lower-case; he is simply pressing a key with the first letter of his name. However, in reality Robert is learning a whole range of skills:

- the sound 'r' has two symbols: 'R' and 'r';
- the space bar is used to separate letters and eventually words;
- backspace is used to make corrections and the return key to move down;
- discipline, to produce work accurately (since only accuracy is rewarded by a printout to take home).

The use of the 'caps' key is not important at this stage; just continue to teach the pupil to type his name one letter at a time:

ro ro ro ro ro ro ro ro ro ro
ro ro ro ro ro ro ro ro ro ro

then:

rob rob rob rob rob rob rob, etc.

NB: Saying the letter out loud as it is pressed reinforces the action. Also, the pupil should be using the correct finger for the left or right side of the keyboard so 'r' is pressed with the left index finger and 'o' is pressed with the right index finger.

When the first name has been learned, the surname can be taught in the same way. Once he/she can type both names accurately, teach the use of the caps key, or how to operate the shift key with the other hand, since this is more time efficient.

Limit the amount of practice time to 5–10 minutes per day, to prevent boredom. Providing a printout usually maintains motivation.

When appropriate, proceed to teaching the pupil's address. Additionally, words from the National Literacy reading/spelling lists can be used to reinforce placement of letters, as well as improve access times, e.g.:

> **the the the the the the the the the**
> **the the the the the the the the the,** etc.

For older pupils it would be more appropriate to use high frequency words including some subject-specific vocabulary for typing practice. Use the same method as above and limit practice to 10–15 minutes per day.

Additional considerations:

- If necessary, use a card 'mask' over the keyboard and cut out the letters one at a time as they are introduced. Remember to cut out gaps for the space bar and return key, to reduce the distraction of other keys and improve concentration on the task.
- Occasionally co-ordination is so poor that the pupil needs a keyguard, which may be used with/without a mask, as appropriate.
- Raising the back of the keyboard, or using an angled board, as required, helps the pupil to see the keys more clearly.
- Use a standard word processing package unless the pupil needs auditory feedback to reinforce letter sounds and aid spelling. Many classrooms have **'Talking First Word'**, or a useful alternative is **'Write:Outloud'**. **'First Keys 2'** also supports the English curriculum and helps to develop keyboard skills.
- If the pupil has problems with the auto-repeat feature, switch it off from the Settings menu (*Control Panel – Keyboard – Speed*).

Teaching touch typing skills

Once the pupil is a proficient two-finger typist and if writing is still developing slowly or there are problems with either legibility or production of work, consider the option of teaching touch typing.

Advantages

The pupil:

- can achieve higher speeds of typing with motivation and practice (over 40 wpm);
- does not have to look repeatedly from screen to keyboard;
- can type from text/notes/whiteboard with greater ease;
- learns the *pattern* of words with fingers on the keyboard (in the same way that the hand learns the pattern when you develop cursive script, aiding spelling);
- learns a transferable skill with possibly greater opportunities in workplace.

Disadvantages

Pupils have to:

- learn to use all fingers with equal dexterity;
- learn which fingers match which keys;
- persevere with exercises which may appear boring since it takes some time to develop accuracy and speed.

Pre-skills

Staff need to check that pupils can:

- isolate each finger – can the pupil touch each finger to thumb?
- understand the movements up, down, left/right, etc. in relation to the keyboard.

Method:

- Use the same principles as mentioned in teaching two-fingered typing, i.e. short teaching sessions and printouts, to maintain motivation.
- The aim is reasonable proficiency in producing work; complete accuracy may not be achieved, or even achievable.
- Learning to touch type requires a degree of commitment and understanding that it takes time for the skill to become automatic.

Resources:

1. *Keyboarding Skills for Children with Disabilities* by Dorothy Penso, published by Whurr (also appropriate for other pupils).

This gives practice in *vertical letter patterns* formed by each finger on the keyboard (i.e. left index finger presses 'frfvf'), as opposed to the usual *horizontal patterns* (left-hand fingers press 'asdf'). This is particularly useful with pupils who have co-ordination difficulties and problems with spatial awareness.

2. Computer programs are available from a number of suppliers (Resources, page 130).

'Speedy Keys' – develops familiarity with the keyboard, good graphics and incorporates National Literacy Strategy word lists.

'TypeQuick for Students' is an interactive adventure in 10 structured lessons that motivate pupils to learn to touch type.

'Ultrakey 4' is a clear and easy to use TT programme which is very popular in the USA and Canada. It provides lots of feedback, good graphics and allows the teacher to customise the programme for each pupil.

'Touch Type' is a standard on-screen typing tutor for school-aged pupils. This is adaptable for pupils with special needs.

'Success with Typing' (from TypeQuick) has good graphics and lessons which can be tailored to the individual's needs.

'Mavis Beacon Teaches TT' is one of the standard commercially produced programmes available, but this may progress too quickly for younger pupils.

Early keyboard skills checklist

Name: .... DOB: ....

Skill	Begun	Mastered	Programs used
1. Understands cause and effect (e.g. programs using space bar)			
2. Types first name unaided			
3. Uses space bar/return & delete key			
4. Uses number line			
5. Uses number line/return & space bar			
6. Uses arrow keys			
7. Types full name unaided			
8. Uses caps lock/shift key			
9. Copy types a sentence			
10. Uses full stop			
11. Speed increasing			
Mouse skills			
1. Can single-click on a large object			
2. Draws simple picture using shapes			
3. Can single-click on a small object			
4. Produces more detailed picture			
5. Can 'click & drag' in a program			
6. Can click & drag on the desktop			
7. Can double-click			
Computer control			
1. Can switch on and log on			
2. Can switch off correctly			
3. Can open own folder of work			
4. Can select and open programs			

Keyboard shortcuts and use of menus	Begun	Mastered	Programs used
1. Can print own work 　a. using Ctrl + P 　b. using Print from menu bar			
2. Can save work 　a. Ctrl + S 　b. from menu bar			
3. Can open a new file 　a. Ctrl + O 　b. from menu bar			
4. Can quit from the program 　a. Alt + F4 　b. from the menu bar			
5. Can 'select all' text 　a. Ctrl + A 　b. from the Edit menu			
6. Can change font (Font menu)			
7. Can highlight text using click & drag			
8. Can format work selecting 　a. **bold** (Ctrl + B) 　b. *italic* (Ctrl + I) 　c. underline (Ctrl + U)			
9. Can change font size 　a. from font bar 　b. Ctrl + Shift + > or <			
10. Can use Ctrl + C to copy text			
11. Can use Ctrl + V to paste text			
12. Can use Ctrl + X to delete text			
13. Can create new folder 　a. from right-hand click menu 　b. Ctrl + N			
14. Can save work to own folder			
15. Can 'save as' using F12 key			
16. Can close window using Ctrl + W			
17. Can use Ctrl + Z to undo			

Teaching dictation skills

For some pupils, e.g. those with severe dyspraxia/dyslexia, or those whose written work does not reflect their level of knowledge, the most effective means of recording work may be by dictation. This is especially important for those approaching examinations at secondary level.

Dictating work, whether to a support assistant or using word recognition software, requires a level of skill, experience and self-discipline. It is important that the support assistant does not anticipate the answer, extending or improving sentences, since the aim is to provide evidence of the pupil's level of attainment.

Additionally, to get good grades in examinations, pupils need to show the planning of an essay, since this can add marks if there is insufficient time to finish a question.

Pupils need to develop a series of skills in the following sequence:

Stage:	To move to the next stage:
The pupil dictates: ❏ short phrases; ❏ longer phrases with 'and' links; ❏ grammatically correct short sentences; ❏ longer grammatically correct sentences with one linking word, e.g. and, but, however, although; ❏ sentences, showing how to indicate 'new sentence', 'full stop', 'comma', 'new paragraph'.	• discuss re-drafting and ask 'who did what?', 'when/where/why?'; • go over work and ask pupil to break it up into shorter sentences based on the above; • use set/created Clicker grids to demonstrate links and sentence structure; • use 'story starts' and picture sequences to extend sentences; • read the pupil's work back and ask him/her to note breath pauses (full stop) and shorter pauses (comma), make it a game; • give the pupil a passage with no punctuation and ask him/her to punctuate.
Planning answers **Can the pupil:** ❏ sequence a series of sentences describing an activity? ❏ identify the beginning, middle and end of a story? ❏ plan a short story by giving main points, written on Post-its, and organising these into an answer?	• use set/prepared Clicker grids; • give longer passages which have been cut up and ask the pupil to sequence them; • use software, e.g. 'Kidspiration', or

Teaching scissors skills

Prerequisites

The pupil must be able to:
- open and close the hand;
- use both hands together, with the dominant hand leading and the other hand assisting;
- isolate or combine the movements of thumb, index and middle fingers;
- co-ordinate arm, hand and eye movements;
- stabilise the wrist, elbow and shoulder joints to provide a base for hand movements;
- show evidence of imitating cutting movements in play situations.

Pre-scissors activities	
Pick-up games Resources: • a bucket or container; • salad servers, sugar tongs, etc.; • a variety of small objects, e.g. cotton/aluminium foil balls, plastic toys, bells, bricks.	Objectives: • the pupil has to pick up objects and carry them to the bucket/container; • gradually increase the distance.
Squeeze play Resources: • squirt guns, bulb-squeezers, turkey basters, etc.; • balloons, washing-up liquid.	Objectives: • the pupil has to squirt water into a bowl of soapy water to make bubbles; • the pupil has to squirt water at balloons hanging from a line to make them move.
Paper-punch games Resources: • paper punch; • stiff paper/thin card; • laces/crayons.	Objectives: • the pupil makes random holes in the paper/card with the punch and then joins the holes with laces/crayon marks; • draw a path on a piece of card and ask the pupil to punch holes along the path.

Activities such as scrunching tissue/thin/thick paper, tearing it into random pieces then strips, etc. also help to develop bi-manual hand control.

Holding the scissors correctly:

- The pupil should place the thumb and middle fingers through the scissor loops.
- The index finger stabilises the scissors resting just above the lower loop (see right).

Simplifying the cutting task

To teach cutting along a straight line – ask the pupil to:
- cut along a line of punched holes (reducing task into a series of small snips);
- cut between two lolly sticks stuck on the paper;
- cut along the edge of a piece of card stuck on the paper;
- cut through the middle of a line of small stickers on the paper;
- cut along a line drawn with a thick marker pen.

To teach cutting out a circle – ask the pupil to:
- cut around a circle of punched holes;
- cut around the edge of a round piece of card stuck on the paper;
- cut out the circle in sections (the template looks like a radiating sun);
- cut around a circle of small stickers on the paper;
- cut around a circle drawn with a thick marker pen.

Resources

Low muscle tone/limited physical ability may result in poor scissors skills. The main difficulty is opening the scissors blades once they are closed. Scissors are available which reduce this problem. All the self-opening scissors shown below have safety caps in place.

Types of scissors	Comments:	
Foundation Stage		
Fiskars Nursery 'Squeezar'	• snipping action only	
Small 'Easy Grip'	• single loop requiring squeeze action	
Fiskars Safety	• plastic blades	
KS1 and KS2		
Teaching scissors (right- or left-handed)	• two holes in each handle	
'Easy Grip' Right- and left-handed self-opening	• single loop requiring squeeze action • spring-loaded action	
Longloop right- and left-handed self-opening	• all four fingers used in lower grip	
Longloop right- and left-handed (not shown)	• all four fingers used in lower grip	
Fiskars Junior right- and left-handed	• larger lower loop	

Scissors skills checklist

Stage	Developmental Stage	Date Achieved
1.	The pupil shows an interest in scissors	
2.	The pupil holds and manipulates scissors appropriately	
3.	The pupil opens and closes scissors in a controlled fashion	
4.	The pupil makes random snips	
5.	The pupil manipulates the scissors in a forward motion	
	✂ cuts across a 2 cm strip of thin card in any fashion	
	✂ cuts across a 5 cm strip of thin card in any fashion	
	✂ cuts across a 10 cm strip of thin card in any fashion	
	✂ cuts across a 20 cm strip of thin card in any fashion	
6.	The pupil begins to control the forward movement of the scissors	
	✂ cuts across paper, staying within a 15 cm line	
	✂ cuts across paper, staying within a 10 cm line	
	✂ cuts across paper, staying within a 5 cm line	
	✂ cuts across paper, staying within a 2 cm line	
7.	The pupil cuts along a straight line accurately	
	✂ cuts along a thick line made with a marker pen	
	✂ cuts along a thinner line made with a marker pen	
8.	The pupil cuts simple geometric shapes	
	✂ cuts out a square or oblong	
	✂ cuts out a triangle	
	✂ cuts out a semicircle	
	✂ cuts out a circle	
9.	The pupil cuts out simple figure shapes	
10.	The pupil cuts out complex figure shapes	
11.	The pupil cuts non-paper materials	

Date begun: ....

Comments: ....

....

....

....

Independence skills

9 months	• holds, bites, chews small pieces of food; • puts hands around bottle or cup when feeding; • tries to grasp spoon when being fed.
1 year	• drinks from cup with little assistance; • holds spoon and attempts to use for feeding (very messy); • helps with dressing by holding out arm for sleeve, foot for shoe.
15 months	• holds a cup and drinks without assistance; • holds spoon, brings to mouth and licks it but unable to stop it turning over; • chews well; • helps with dressing.
18 months	• holds spoon, gets food safely to mouth but may still play with food; • lifts and holds cup in both hands, drinks independently but hands empty cup to adult; • assists with dressing, takes off own hat, shoes and socks but seldom able to replace; • indicates urgent toilet needs by restlessness and vocalisation; • bowel control may be attained but variable; • may indicate wet or soiled pants.
2 years	• eats independently with a spoon but is easily distracted; • puts on hat and shoes; • usually attempts to say toilet needed in sufficient time, still unreliable.
2½ years	• eats skilfully with a spoon and may use a fork; • pulls pants down when using the toilet but seldom able to replace them; • may be dry through the night but this is variable.
3 years	• washes hands but needs help with drying; • can eat with a spoon and sometimes a fork; • can pull pants up and down, needs help with fastenings; • is clean and dry in the day, almost reliable at night (variable).
4 years	• eats skilfully with spoon and fork; • dresses, undresses independently besides laces, ties, back buttons; • can wipe own bottom; • can wash and dry hands.
5 years	• eats competently using a knife and fork; • dresses and undresses independently; • washes and dries hands and face but needs supervision for the rest.

Reference

Adapted from Sheridan, M. (2003) From Birth to Five Years, Routledge.

Developing self-help skills

Dressing skills:

- Encourage the pupil to use a long mirror. Play games to develop awareness of body size and shape.
- Develop movements for putting clothes on, e.g. quoits over wrists, ankles and hoops up to the waist and over the head, before practising dressing skills.
- Play games to practise skills, e.g. dressing up with large clothes in the house corner.
- Backward chaining would be a useful method to teach the putting on of items of clothing, e.g. putting on trousers:
    - help pupil put trousers on up to knees; pupil pulls the trousers up independently;
    - help pupil put trousers on up to ankles; pupil pulls trousers up independently;
    - help pupil put one leg in; pupil continues;
    - pupil is shown how to lay trousers out and put them on;
    - pupil sits and puts trousers on independently.
- Practise doing fasteners on dolls which have large buttons, zips and Velcro fastenings, do laces on wooden shoeboxes or tie up parcels.
- Encourage parents to dress their child in shoes with Velcro fastenings, trousers/skirts with elasticated waist, school ties on elastic, clothes which are not tight (it may be necessary for uniform to have modifications to accommodate this).
- Younger pupils may benefit from having all their belongings, bags, hats in a particular colour, in order for them to be found more easily in the cloakroom.
- Provide cue cards or lists to show what order clothes are taken off/put on.

| Trousers | T-shirt | Trainers | Jumper |

Putting on clothes in this order:

- Encourage sitting to dress/undress, sitting with the back to a solid surface or holding onto a chair back to aid balance.
- Use T-shirts/sweatshirts with a logo/design on the front to help orientation of clothes.
- Give praise for effort when the pupil is trying to dress independently.
- Only help the pupil when he/she has tried for him-/herself.
- Ensure the pupil does not miss out on playtime, etc. if he/she is slow to dress.

Older pupils:

- Older pupils need to develop coping strategies to overcome their difficulties.
- Clothes need to be considered carefully to enable the pupil to have credibility with his/her peers. Consider how fashions can be adapted to make dressing easier.

- Adapt clothes with elastic, Velcro®, e.g. cut the school tie and join with Velcro®, adapt cuffs by putting in elastic to allow the hand to fit through.
- Use 'curly laces', wear polo shirts, jumpers with logos to help orientation, jumpers with raglan sleeves, wear belts with a magnetic buckle.

Independent toileting:

- Parents should be encouraged to dress their child in clothes that are easy to pull up and down.
- Prompt cards can help to develop independent routines.
- Wet wipes should be available for pupils who find it difficult to cleanse themselves.
- Mirrors in a strategic position can help the pupil to check that he/she has thoroughly cleansed themselves.

Personal appearance:

- Pupils may be unaware of their appearance, making them vulnerable to teasing.
- Encourage pupils to check appearance in mirrors placed in toilets.

Eating

Pupils with co-ordination difficulties may find it difficult to develop good eating habits. Younger pupils often dislike foods with variable textures, find it difficult to manipulate cutlery, preferring to finger-feed, and may have poor oral skills which makes chewing more difficult. This may continue to cause difficulties as pupils get older.

Younger pupils:

- Play with spoons to scoop sand, shaving foam, imitation peas.
- Practise using plastic knives and forks to cut playdough, clay, etc.
- Some pupils with co-ordination difficulties may not easily tolerate food at extremes of temperatures and may not like combinations of textures of food on a plate, e.g. meat, vegetables and gravy.
- Encourage parents to practise feeding at home:
  - give food which can be 'stabbed' with a fork;
  - use a knife to slice soft foods, e.g. banana, progressing to harder foods;
  - use a spoon and fork with soft foods;
  - carry out activities which use two hands together, e.g. peeling a banana.
- Use Dycem to stabilise dishes.
- Moulded cutlery helps place fingers in the correct place.
- Adapted cutlery with built-up handles can help pupils with weak wrists.

Developing coping strategies:

Some pupils may always find it difficult to eat appropriately and may need encouragement to develop coping strategies:

- Select food which is easier to eat, e.g. mashed potato rather than spaghetti.
- Have a packed lunch rather than a cooked meal.
- Have a tissue/wet wipe in the lunch box or pocket, to wipe the face after eating.
- Have a small mirror in the lunch box or pocket to check that the face is clean.

Dressing skills progression and checklist

Children acquire dressing skills in a hierarchical manner. Some children with co-ordination difficulties will take longer to develop these skills, but when teaching they should still be addressed in the order below.

Approximate age	Skill development
1 year	❑ co-operates in dressing, e.g. holds foot up for shoe to be put on; ❑ puts hat on head; ❑ takes off socks.
2 years	❑ has the prerequisite skills to lift arms above the head and maintain balance; ❑ pulls off an unfastened coat, tries to put on socks, tries to pull down trousers; ❑ tries to put on a coat; ❑ finds armholes in a T-shirt; ❑ unbuttons a large button.
3 years	❑ perceptually aware of more details, e.g. where armholes are; ❑ improved balance when sitting while reaching above the head; ❑ is able to reach behind the back; ❑ pulls down trousers, skirts independently; ❑ can put on socks and shoes; ❑ can put on front-fastening garments; ❑ requires help with T-shirts; ❑ is able to fasten large buttons, pull up zips.
4 years	❑ behind the back co-ordination develops; ❑ can remove a T-shirt, jumper; ❑ can fasten buckles and fasten a separating zip; ❑ is able to put on socks, shoes; ❑ can distinguish between the front and back of clothes.
5 years	❑ is able to balance; ❑ puts on a jumper, T-shirt correctly orientated; ❑ can now dress unsupervised.
6 years	❑ can tie laces; ❑ can fasten buttons behind the back.
8 years	❑ has the ability to select the correct clothes for the weather.
10 years	❑ can tie a necktie.

Reference
Adapted from Dunn Klein, M. (1983) Pre-Dressing Skills, Winslow Press.

Teaching dressing skills

The child with co-ordination difficulties frequently struggles to take off and put on his/her coat and shoes, and change for PE. Dressing skills should be:

- taught in a hierarchical order (see Dressing skill progression page 90);
- taught using the backward chaining method, where the child completes the final small step of the task;
- carried out with the child in a stable position, e.g. by sitting on a chair, on the floor with the back resting against the wall;
- practised with oversized garments before using actual clothing.

Taking shoes off	**Putting shoes on**
1. The child takes hold of a single lace or the Velcro strap and loosens it;	1. The child holds the shoe open, pushes the tongue back;
2. pulls the tongue of the shoe forward then pushes the shoe off, using the other foot or by hand.	2. pushes the foot into the shoe (it might help to place the toe of the shoe against a hard surface).

Taking socks off	**Putting socks on**
1. The child tucks the thumbs into the top of the sock;	1. The child holds the sock open at the top and folds it over slightly;
2. pushes the sock down past the heel;	2. hooks his/her thumbs in the top and places it over the big toe;
3. holds the toe end and pulls it off.	3. pulls it up over the heel.

Taking a jumper off
(same method can be used for T-shirts and coats)

1. The child grasps the collar or neck at the back of the garment, pulls it over the head while keeping the head down;

2. pulls one arm out (weaker side first) then pulls out the other arm.

Putting a jumper on

1. The child lays the jumper out on the table or lap with the back uppermost and the opening nearest the tummy;

2. pushes one arm into the sleeve, making sure the hand comes right out of the cuff (weaker arm in first); repeats with other arm;

3. leans forward, tucks the chin down and pulls the jumper over the head.

Putting a coat on

1. The child lays the coat on the table or lap with the lining uppermost and the hood or collar next to the tummy;

2. pushes one arm into the sleeve, making sure the hand comes out of the cuff (weaker side first); repeats with the other arm;

3. stretches out the arms and lifts them over the head keeping the chin tucked down;

4. sits up straight and wriggles to make the coat fall into place on the back.

Taking trousers off

Putting trousers on

(same method can be used for shorts and pants)

If the child's standing balance is insecure, encourage him/her to hold onto a static object or sit down.

1. The child tucks thumbs into the waistband;

2. pushes the trousers down over the hips and knees, holding on with one hand;

3. or sits down and pushes the trousers down over the feet.

1. The child sits on a chair;

2. or on the floor to put legs in;

3. rolls from side to side, pulling trousers up over the hips;

4. or sits on the chair then stands holding on with one hand as in picture 2 opposite centre.

Communication and social skills

Some pupils with co-ordination difficulties may have problems with communication skills. The following suggestions may support these pupils.

Foundation Stage

Difficulty	Strategies
Plays alone rather than in a group	<ul><li>set up play situations for two children involving turn-taking, support the play with explicit words, Sam's turn, Amy's turn (build up the number of children in the group);</li><li>support the interaction of the pupil at playtime with adult-led games, e.g. 'Ring-a-Ring o' Roses'.</li></ul>
Lack of imaginative play	<ul><li>model play in the 'house' corner;</li><li>support play in model-making areas.</li></ul>
Difficulty following simple routines and instructions	<ul><li>use a visual timetable with simple photographs, to show the routine of the session (in an individual format or for the whole class);</li><li>give simple instructions, one at a time;</li><li>support instructions with visual prompts: e.g. point to where the item should be placed when gluing; model activities;</li><li>use 'hand-over-hand' movements to demonstrate what is expected;</li><li>play games which encourage listening skills, e.g. simplified version of 'Simon Says'.</li></ul>
Unclear speech	<ul><li>ask the family to check with the GP regarding possible hearing problems;</li><li>possible speech and language therapy (SALT) assessment required;</li><li>encourage participation in singing rhymes, copying rhythms with musical instruments;</li><li>encourage use of non-verbal language: gestures, pictures, signs to accompany speech;</li><li>give choices in a sentence which require a short response rather than a long one, e.g. 'Do you want to play with the garage or the bricks?', as this requires a short answer rather than an attempt at a whole sentence;</li><li>praise and respond to attempts to communicate.</li></ul>
Poor eye contact	<ul><li>sit facing the pupil when working/playing together;</li><li>hold objects which are being discussed, up to the face, to encourage looking at the speaker.</li></ul>

Primary pupils

Difficulty	Strategies
Poor eye contact	• encourage by comment 'look at my face'; • seat opposite rather than alongside when working with the pupil.
Daydreams	• seat close to the teacher for whole-class input; • place in a work area which is as distraction-free as possible (away from windows, displays); • give gentle prompts (written or spoken) to encourage a return to task.
Poor articulation, difficulty organising speech	• SALT input; • reduce pressure on the pupil; it may be better to avoid questioning in large groups; • give cues if word finding is a problem, e.g. give the initial sound of the word; • use a home/school book for parents to say what has been done at home to help the pupil at news time; school to show what has been achieved, in order for the pupil to talk about what has been done at school.
Slow to process information and give feedback, either verbal or physical	• allow time to respond to questions, instructions; • avoid unnecessary words in instructions; • keep instructions short and to the point and give in the order that the activity is to take place; • ask the pupil to vocalise what he/she has to do; • put instructions for work to be completed on the board; • use cue cards as prompts to start/finish an activity; • minimise background noise when giving instructions.
Develops avoidance strategies	• give positive feedback, support difficult activities, provide alternative recording strategies. • see Promoting self-esteem (page 99).
Asks 'never-ending' questions	• have a rule: only one answer will be given to a question; • be prepared to repeat an instruction and give written/verbal support to the pupil when he/she is beginning a task; • give praise when a task is being carried out in order to provide reassurance.

Secondary pupils

Difficulty	Strategies
Unable to follow complex instructions	• have instructions for the lesson on the board or printed out; • ensure instructions for homework are understood; give a slip of paper with them on to take home.
Difficulty sequencing events, particularly in written format	• give picture cues or written prompts when writing up an experiment; • encourage the use of storyboards for story writing.
Poor speech production	• avoid asking questions in a large group; • refrain from asking the pupil to read aloud if he/she is uncomfortable with this.
Social isolation	• use buddy systems; • give opportunities to learn about social skills: giving eye contact, listening to the other speakers, giving them time to talk; • encourage and support group working; • encourage the pupil to take part in school clubs; • have designated areas, e.g. SEN areas which provide a quiet place for pupils who lack the social skills to cope at lunchtimes; • have supervised activities, e.g. card games which help to develop social skills.
Pre-occupation with topics or subjects	• channel the pupil's pre-occupation with particular interests into topic work where possible; • teach that it is only appropriate to talk about one's particular interests for a certain length of time; • use pupil's interests to support others, e.g. teaching computer skills if that is the particular interest.

Promoting self-esteem

Pupils may have a poor self-image for a number of reasons:

- They may feel incompetent and frustrated because of difficulties in carrying out day-to-day tasks, resulting in inappropriate behaviour or becoming withdrawn.
- Pupils with co-ordination difficulties may have difficulties relating to their peers for a number of reasons:
    - having unco-ordinated movements which result in their bumping into others, knocking over their equipment, etc.;
    - lacking gross motor skills, so that they do not get picked for teams at playtime and in PE lessons;
    - having a poor tactile system which results in rough play;
    - having inappropriate social skills;
    - being vulnerable to bullying;
    - being perceived by their peers as someone who cannot write neatly, draw well, cut neatly, eat their food appropriately, etc.
- Pupils may be perceived inappropriately, i.e. lazy, naughty.
- Adolescent growth spurts can make problems worse; pupils have to develop co-ordination over again.

Strategies to develop pupils' self-esteem:

- The teacher should be a good role model to other pupils in the class, in respect to the pupil with co-ordination difficulties, by showing understanding of the pupil's difficulties rather than by being irritated by them.
- In the Foundation Stage:
    - give play opportunities to encourage appropriate interaction with peers, e.g. supporting imaginative play in the home corner, offering turn-taking games;
    - offer construction-type toys which are easier to manipulate, e.g. 'Clic' wooden pieces which connect press stud fastenings, 'Stickle bricks', 'Magnetic blocks' shapes, which connect easily with magnets. Encourage and support this type of play.
- Provide activities which are at the appropriate level to avoid frustration.
- Identify areas of difficulty and use a small-steps approach to interventions.
- Allow pupils to compete against themselves rather than be in competition with their peers.
- Set up gross motor groups to improve motor co-ordination, which provide success (see page 47).
- Provide alternative recording strategies which allow the pupil to produce some attractive pieces of work (see page 76).
- Acknowledge that a much greater effort is required to complete a task than for some other pupils and praise accordingly, rather than making comments such as 'hurry up', 'work faster'.

- Mark work according to content rather than appearance.

- Use circle time to focus on strengths.

- Observe the pupil at breaktimes to ascertain isolation. If so, set up buddy systems and alternatives to playtime, e.g. encourage pupils to work on a computer together. Introduce games supported by older pupils or dinner supervisors.

- Introduce games in the playground which are supported by a classroom assistant, lunchtime supervisor or older pupils.

- Encourage coping strategies, e.g. providing a packed lunch which is easily eaten, instead of a cooked lunch, which may allow poor eating habits to be revealed.

- Support the pupil to develop organisational skills, so that he/she does not disrupt or annoy other pupils, e.g. avoid spreading into another pupil's working area, by marking out a working area and encourage staying within it. Provide storage into which pupils can put belongings and encourage sorting it out regularly.

- It may be possible to set up situations where a pupil is able to demonstrate strengths and teach another pupil, e.g. how to use a new game on the computer.

- Give the pupil responsibility, e.g. carrying out jobs within the classroom.

- Use a buddy system to support appropriate movement around school.

- Be aware that some pupils may be easily led as they may take language literally and do as their peers tell them.

- Some pupils could be vulnerable to teasing and bullying, which would need to be addressed.

Personal organisation

Preparing for secondary transfer

Moving to a new school can be daunting for any pupil especially those with co-ordination and organisational difficulties. The following suggestions are intended to help prepare pupils for a successful transition period.

Area of concern	Suggestions
Sharing information with the new school	• primary schools will automatically share information with the receiving school; • parents can arrange to meet with the SENCO at the new school before their child transfers to discuss individual needs or concerns; • parents should put their points in writing to make sure everything is covered during the meeting.
Getting to know the building	• ask for a plan of the new school; ask for information about one-way systems in corridors and stairs; find out how lunchtime is organised; • try to help your child familiarise him-/herself with the layout of the building; • try to attend open evenings with your child before the new term begins; • ensure that your child is present during preparation visits organised by the primary school; • request additional visits for your child if you think this would be helpful; • when timetables are distributed encourage your child to colour-code each subject and cross-reference this to colour-coded rooms on the school building plan.
Organising personal belongings	• prepare three timetables using a computer if possible: one to show lessons, one to show equipment needed and one for homework; colour-code each one; • back or cover exercise and textbooks in a colour that corresponds with the timetable and school plan; • purchase a set of clear plastic wallets to organise all the books and equipment needed for each subject; • if possible, duplicate pencil, pen and ruler in each wallet as this will reduce the need for organising writing equipment at the beginning and end of each lesson; • always check that the school bag is packed the night before; • provide lunch money on a daily basis, if required.

Keeping up with written work	• if a computer is available and keyboard skills are weak, try to provide extra practice so that a computer can be used for longer pieces of written work, both at home and at school; • try to monitor exercise books and watch out for comments about unfinished work; make an appointment to discuss any concerns with the SENCO.
Managing homework	• if your child has difficulties remembering what is required for homework, ask for support from the school: this could include homework slips prepared by the teacher, homework written in the diary by an adult, teacher checking the homework diary to ensure it has been completed, use of a Dictaphone to record homework, homework being circulated by email; homework being posted on the school website; • allow your child to have a short rest and a drink and snack before starting homework; • encourage your child to take regular short breaks between subjects to aid concentration; • make sure you are aware of the school homework policy and monitor how long your child is spending on each subject; • discuss concerns with the SENCO or individual subject teachers; • encourage your child to use homework clubs if available.

Suggestions for teenagers

Revising for exams

Some suggestions which may help you to be successful:

- Revise with a friend, talk ideas through together.
- Break your notes up into sections, rather than trying to revise a large section at once.
- Use all your senses; listen to tapes (made by yourself or commercial ones), read notes, watch videos, write out what you have learned using highlighter pens to mark the main points.
- Have plenty of drinks of water and eat dried fruit, apricots, etc. while you are working.
- Try to find silly ways to remember things.
- Plan to give yourself a reward when you have done the revision you needed to do.
- Your school may be able to gain extra time for you to do your exams.

Sports activities outside school

When choosing a sports activity, consider:

- Team games require co-ordination of a lot of movements, quick responses, and may also involve pressure from other team members and be more difficult to take part in.
- Activities such as aerobics, line dancing require a sequence of movements and a faster response, which can prove disheartening when it is difficult to keep up.
- Solitary sports such as weight building, golf, fishing, horse riding give time to think and respond and may be more satisfying.
- Those activities which allow for self-competition can boost self-esteem: activities in the gym, running, golf, swimming.
- Try badminton, tennis, table tennis, etc. with a non-competitive friend.
- Aquarobics, Pilates and yoga provide slower forms of exercise and promote relaxation.
- Some activities can help to improve co-ordination: judo, karate, archery and snooker; swimming helps to build up strength on both sides of the body.

Hobbies

Developing a satisfying hobby can be a good form of relaxation, a way of socialising if carried out at a class or club, and a way to boost self-esteem. Some enjoyable hobbies may be:

- listening to music, which can be relaxing;
- playing an instrument, which requires the correct choice of instrument to ensure that it is not a cause of frustration;
- working with clay, which makes less exacting demands than other craft activities;
- creative writing (using a word processor);
- photography, which can produce satisfying results;
- playing draughts or chess, which develops memory and planning.

Organising yourself at home/school

Some suggestions for making life easier:

- Use a large diary to write a list of things to be done; an electronic organiser could help.

- Use Post-it notes in the bedroom, etc. for reminders of things to take to school, reminders of jobs to be done.

- Have a list of things which may need to be taken to school: bus pass/money, lunch box/lunch money, etc. and pin it near the door; check the night before that you have put everything in your bag.

- Use transparent wallets with a coloured sticker for each subject; put equipment needed for each subject in the folder: matching pencil, exercise book with the same coloured dot.

- Have a rucksack with lots of pockets to store things in, rather than one big holdall where everything disappears in the bottom (tidy it out every day!).

- Have as little extra gear in your bedroom as possible.

- Have labelled boxes, trays to keep stuff in.

- Tidy up every day and have a chocolate bar for doing it!

Further reading and support

'How to Understand and Support Children with Dyspraxia' by Lois Addy (LDA 2003)

'Developmental Co-ordination Disorder: Hints and Tips for the Activities for Daily Living' by Morven F Ball (Jessica Kingsley Publishers 2002)

'Praxis Makes Perfect' by Sidney Chu (available from the Dyspraxia Foundation)

'Living with Dyspraxia: A Guide for Adults with Developmental Dyspraxia' compiled by Mary Colley (Dyspraxia Foundation 2002)

'Pre-Writing Skills: Skill Starters for Motor Development' by Marsha Dunn Klein (Communication Skill Builders 1982)

'Pre-Dressing Skills' by Marsha Dunn Klein (Winslow Press 1983)

'Pre-Scissor Skills' by Marsha Dunn Klein (Winslow Press 1987)

'Assessing Communication' by Clare Latham and Ann Miles (David Fulton Publishers 1997)

'Dyspraxia in the Early Years' by Christine Macintyre (David Fulton Publishers 2000)

'Keyboarding Skills for Children with Disabilities' by Dorothy Penso (Whurr Publishers 1999)

'Handwriting: A Second Chance' by Philomena Pickard (LDA)

'Developmental Dyspraxia: A Practical Manual for Parents and Professionals' by Madeleine Portwood (published by Durham County Council)

'Developmental Dyspraxia: Identification and Intervention – A Manual for Parents and Professionals' by Madeleine Portwood (David Fulton Publishers 1999)

'Understanding Developmental Dyspraxia: A Textbook for Students and Professionals' by Madeleine Portwood (David Fulton Publishers 2000)

'Ready Steady – Go To PE! Assessment and Activities for Early Gross Motor Skills: A Practical Guide for Teachers' by ReLEASS (Regional LEA Support Services) (available from ESPD at Frederick Holmes School, Inglemire Lane, Hull HU6 8JJ)

'Dyspraxia: A Guide for Teachers and Parents' by Kate Ripley, Bob Daines and Jenny Barrett (David Fulton Publishers 1997)

'Spontaneous Play in Early Childhood: From Birth to Six Years' by Mary Sheridan (Routledge 1999)

'From Birth to Five Years: Children's Developmental Progress' by Mary Sheridan, Revised and updated by Marion Frost and Dr Ajay Sharma (Routledge 2003)

'Write from the Start' by Prof. Teodorescu and Lois Addy (LDA)

'Supporting Children with Communication Problems' by Jannet A. Wright and Myra Kersner (David Fulton Publishers 1998)

Management issues

These are whole-school issues to be considered by the senior management team when planning to meet the needs of a pupil with co-ordination difficulties.

Consideration	Yes	No	Action required
Are the governors aware of their responsibilities in ensuring that the needs of pupils with co-ordination difficulties are met?			
Are all staff aware of the educational implications of co-ordination difficulties?			
Is there a need for additional adult support for the pupil?			
Are staff appropriately trained?			
Is there effective communication between home and school in place?			
Are other agencies involved in meeting the needs of the pupil?			
Do you know where to seek further information and advice?			
Are you aware of recent legislation, LEA/SEN policies?			
Are there strategies to support the child's emotional well-being?			
Are there strategies to promote positive peer-group relationships?			
Do you promote positive images of the child?			
Are appropriate teaching strategies in place?			
Are any additional resources required to support curriculum delivery?			

Pupil Profile 1

Name: .... Class: .... Date:................

Area of development	Observed difficulties (Foundation Stage)
Sensory	❏ very excitable, making shrill or loud noises, hand flapping; ❏ cannot sit still during circle or story time; ❏ limited concentration, flitting from one activity to another; ❏ distressed by high levels of noise; ❏ dislikes being touched or avoids certain textures; ❏ fiddles, chews objects or clothes; ❏ poor safety awareness or a fear of heights; ❏ fussy eater.
Gross motor skills	❏ clumsy movements, bumps into objects, falls, trips; ❏ easily knocked off-balance; ❏ difficulties climbing on a small climbing frame; ❏ difficulties getting into or onto play equipment and chairs; ❏ jumps from inappropriate heights with no sense of danger; ❏ has to squat to pick up toys from the floor; ❏ difficulties getting up from the floor without using hands; ❏ difficulties jumping with both feet together; ❏ difficulties pedalling a tricycle; ❏ climbs the stairs leading with one foot; ❏ difficulties throwing, catching and kicking a large ball.
Fine motor skills	❏ uncertain of hand dominance; ❏ avoids jigsaws and construction toys; ❏ poor pencil grip; ❏ unable to use scissors; ❏ struggles to build tower of six one-inch cubes.
Independence skills	❏ difficulties taking off coat and hanging it on a peg; ❏ struggles with undressing; ❏ unable to use the toilet independently; ❏ messy eater, prefers to finger-feed; ❏ spills drinks.
Communication	❏ plays alone rather than in a group; ❏ lack of imaginative play; ❏ difficulties following simple routines and instructions; ❏ unclear speech, cannot speak in sentences; ❏ avoidance of eye contact.

Pupil Profile 2

Name: .... Class: .... Date:................

Area of development	Observed difficulties (Key Stages 1 and 2)
Sensory	❏ easily distracted, lacks persistence; ❏ unable to use space effectively in PE or playground; ❏ difficulties judging distance and direction; ❏ difficulties sitting still; ❏ dislikes being touched; ❏ can be rough in play without realising; ❏ irrational fear of open space or heights; ❏ poor self-image, attention-seeking behaviour, withdrawn, underactive, reluctant to participate; ❏ lacks inhibition; ❏ poor visual tracking; ❏ difficulties copying from the board; ❏ dribbles from mouth.
Gross motor skills	❏ awkward, clumsy, bumps into people and objects; ❏ difficulties hopping, jumping, skipping; ❏ poor balance; ❏ poor ball skills; ❏ difficulties learning new tasks or sequences.
Fine motor skills	❏ poor sitting posture; ❏ uncertain of hand dominance; ❏ immature pencil grasp and poor pencil control; ❏ poor drawing skills, messy when using paints; ❏ difficulties using scissors; ❏ avoids handwriting tasks; ❏ difficulties setting out work in books; ❏ unable to construct a model following a diagram or plan.
Independence skills	❏ slow messy eater; ❏ slow to change for PE, mixes up order and orientation of clothes; ❏ avoids using the toilet at school.
Communication	❏ poor eye contact; ❏ daydreams; ❏ poor articulation, difficulties organising speech; ❏ slow to process information and give feedback (verbal or physical); ❏ develops avoidance strategies; ❏ asks never-ending questions.
Organisation	❏ unable to remember messages; ❏ forgets, cannot find dinner money; ❏ cannot cope with changes of routine; ❏ difficulties selecting equipment for a lesson or activity; ❏ poor sequencing skills.

Pupil Profile 3

Name: .... Class: .... Date:................

Area of development	Observed difficulties (Key Stages 3 and 4)
Sensory	❑ low self-esteem; ❑ little sense of personal safety; ❑ poor road sense as a pedestrian or cyclist; ❑ difficulties coping with board work in class.
Gross motor skills	❑ difficulties in PE and games activities; ❑ reluctant to participate in team games; ❑ evidence of motor stereotypes such as hand-flapping.
Fine motor skills	❑ difficulties keeping up with written work; ❑ books untidy with work being difficult to read and mark; ❑ short written responses which do not match verbal ability; ❑ unable to manipulate ruler, compass, protractor; ❑ struggles in practical subjects.
Independence skills	❑ avoids removing jumper/sweatshirt in very hot weather; ❑ avoids eating with cutlery; ❑ personal hygiene lacks attention.
Communication	❑ unable to follow complex instructions; ❑ difficulties sequencing events, particularly in written format; ❑ poor speech production; ❑ socially isolated; ❑ preoccupied with topics or subjects.
Organisation	❑ carries all belongings for fear of forgetting something; ❑ loses books and writing equipment; ❑ has an unkempt appearance; ❑ encroaches into his/her neighbour's personal space.

Progression of drawing skills

Pupils learn to copy the following shapes in sequential order:

Group 1

Group 2

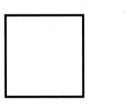

The teaching of handwriting may begin once groups 1 and 2 have been mastered.

Group 3

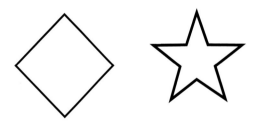

Group 4

NB: Pupils cannot copy a shape in a later group unless they can copy a shape from an earlier group.

Shape copying test

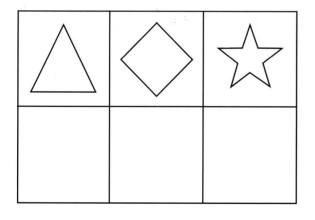

Handwriting assessment form

Name: .... DOB: ....

Tick the appropriate box:

Comments:

1. Sits correctly   Yes ☐   No ☐

2. Handedness   Right ☐   Left ☐

3. Angles paper   Yes ☐   No ☐

4. Fixes with free hand   Yes ☐   No ☐

5. Problems with grasp   Tripod ☐   Immature tripod ☐

                                 Other ☐ ....

6. Pressure   Too much ☐   Too little ☐

7. Incorrect formation   ....
    (e.g. clockwise 'o's) ....
                           ....

8. Reversals of letters   Left/Right   Top/Bottom

9. Erratic sizing   Yes ☐   No ☐

10. Poor alignment   Yes ☐   No ☐

11. Lack of spacing   Yes ☐   No ☐

12. Writing laborious   Yes ☐   No ☐

13. Fluency/speed   Slow ☐   Fast ☐

14. Mixed upper- and   Yes ☐   No ☐
    lower-case

15. Size of writing   Large ☐   Small ☐   Age-appropriate ☐

Poor grasp produces problems in areas 6, 12 and 13. See page 67 if there is a concern.

Strategies to be trialled:

Change in grasp: .... Other: (e.g. 'Write from the Start')
Pen/pencil grip: ....
Pen/pencil: ....
Angled board: ....
Date assessed: .... Reassessment date:..........................

Name: ....

Place drawing here

_____

_____

_____

_____

Date assessed: .... Reassessment date: ....

Handwriting sample 2

Copy the following:

a b c d e f g h i j k l m n o p q r

s t u v w x y z

Check letter formation by copying the following sentence:

The cat sat on the mat.

Place drawing here

Date assessed:.. Reassessment date: ....

Handwriting sample 3

Name: .... Date: ....

Four men and a jolly boy came out of the black and pink house quickly to see the bright violet sun but the sun was behind a cloud.

_____

_____

_____

_____

Speed in letters per minute: ....

Instructions

Ask the pupil to copy the sentence onto the lines above using his/her neatest handwriting. Divide the time taken (remembering to convert seconds into a percentage of a minute) by the number of characters (103). This will give the speed in letters per minute.

Minutes and seconds	%
5 secs	.08
10 secs	.17
15 secs	.25
20 secs	.33
25 secs	.42
30 secs	.50
35 secs	.58
40 secs	.67
45 secs	.75
50 secs	.83
55 secs	.92

Age	Letters per minute
7	20–25
8	30
9	40
10	50
11	60
12	67
13	75
14	80

Handwriting sample 4

Pupil: .... Date: ....

the quick brown fox jumps over the lazy dog

_____

_____

_____

_____

_____

_____

_____

_____

Speed in letters per minute: ....

Instructions

Ask the pupil to copy the sentence as many times as possible in three minutes. Count the number of letters written and divide this total by the number of minutes. Use the table below to determine speed in letters per minute.

Age	Letters per minute
7	54
8	57
9	67
10	81
11	94
12	100
13	115
14	116
15	124
16	133

Number template sample

The arrow indicates the direction in which the number operation is completed.

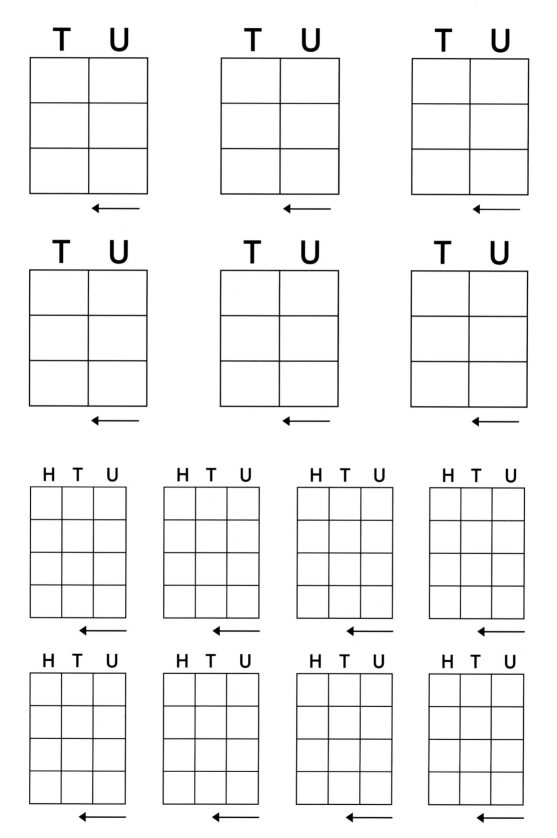

Improving your child's motor co-ordination skills

You can help your child to improve co-ordination skills in a number of ways. However, anything which is done should be fun and not add pressure to yourself or your child.

Younger children

Gross motor skills:

- make family visits to play areas which incorporate ball pools, tunnels, climbing equipment; visit parks with climbing frames, slides over safe flooring;
- walk to school;
- encourage running, jumping, hopping, skipping;
- make obstacle courses through furniture/in the garden, for the child to crawl through;
- play balloon, ball games (choose a ball of the right size and weight that your child can catch);
- play darts with a Velcro board;
- play at catching a ball with the child using a Velcro catcher;
- skittle games;
- make targets: how many times can you throw a beanbag into a waste bin, and improve the targets on a weekly basis; progress by moving the bin further away or by making a smaller target.

Fine motor skills:

- activities to improve hand skills:
  - rolling pastry;
  - playing with playdough;
  - squeezing sponges at bath time;
  - popping bubble wrap;
  - pegging out dolls clothes;
  - finger puppets, finger rhymes;
  - pick-a-stick games;
- provide a variety of pens with different barrels, chalks, large pieces of paper such as lining paper;
- play with toys such as 'Etch a Sketch';
- play drawing games: the parent draws a face shape and encourages the child to put on features (use a mirror to look at features). The same approach can be made when drawing a house or car (pictures may help).

Body awareness:

- ask your child to put bubbles on different parts of the body when playing in the bath;
- naming body parts in pictures in books;
- playing games, e.g. 'Simon Says...', 'Hokey-Cokey';
- playing games in front of a long mirror.

Auditory discrimination:

- play listening games, e.g. 'Grandma Went to Market and Bought...';
- read familiar stories and pause for your child to fill in the missing word or read it incorrectly so that you can be corrected.

Sensory sensitivity:

- improve tactile skills (touch) by introducing finger paints, reading books which have pages with different textures within the story, rolling/crawling on different surfaces, e.g. carpet, hard floor;
- guessing what the toy is in a feely bag before it is pulled out.

Visual perception:

- play matching games: dominoes, snap, pairs;
- jigsaws (with adult help).

Older children

Gross motor skills:

- play 'wheelbarrow' games;
- play push/pull games, tug of war;
- encourage individual sports activities, e.g. body building, golf, judo, swimming rather than team games;
- play swingball;
- practise the skills required in PE lessons in a number of ways: make 'hockey sticks' with rolled up cardboard and play with a foam ball; play tennis with short-handled plastic racquets and soft balls.

Fine motor skills:

- offer a variety of pens with different grips (available from stationers) to see which are easiest and most comfortable to use;
- explore clip art programs to provide alternatives to drawings when illustrating work;
- use templates from art shops to help with science work;
- support model making with Lego.

Visual perception:

- 'dot to dot' books;
- word searches;
- Where's Wally? books;
- play bowls;
- remote control cars.

Remember to praise your child.

Helping your child develop organisational skills

Help your child to become as independent as possible by trying the following ideas:

- Encourage the organisation of equipment needed the next day, before going to bed.
- Use lists for daily checks when packing up personal necessities: dinner money/pack up box, bus passes, etc. (see right); cross through when the item is packed.
- Whiteboards could be used to indicate what happens on each day and the equipment required: Monday is PE day so I need…
- Encourage the tidying up of toys with the use of transparent plastic boxes with picture labels.
- Use boxes which help organisation as your child gets older, e.g. for fishing gear, toiletries.
- Buy a rucksack with pockets, elasticised places to help organisation, rather than a large holdall where everything becomes a muddle.
- Use transparent pencil cases, wallets for reading books, equipment for particular subjects, e.g. protractor, compass, ruler, maths book.
- Ask teachers to check that homework diaries are completed correctly.
- Negotiate the time which should be spent on homework.
- Consider the use of a planner to organise when homework/projects should be done so that completion dates can be met.
- Provide a quiet area to do homework with pens, rubber, ruler to hand.

> **Every day**
> ~~Dinner money~~
> ~~Bus pass~~
> Pencil case
> PE kit
> Planner
>
> **Monday**
> PE kit
>
> **Tuesday**
> Swimming gear
>
> **Wednesday**
> Cookery

Helping your child develop dressing and personal care skills

There are a number of strategies which can be tried to make your child's life easier at school and to encourage his/her independence.

Clothing items which are to be taken to school:

- Choose clothing for your child which will make dressing a little easier and allow more independence: shoes with Velcro fastenings, trousers/skirts with elasticated waistbands (this will help with changing from PE and adjusting clothes after visiting the toilet), clothes which are not tight, e.g. jogging bottoms rather than jeans.
- Put a large, split ring on the top of a coat zip to make it easier to pull up.
- Replace the hanging tab inside the coat with a longer tab made with elastic, which will make it easier to place on a peg.
- Name all your child's belongings with name tabs or indelible ink.
- Have all belongings, e.g. bags, hats, in a particular colour, in order for them to be found more easily in the cloakroom.

Teaching dressing skills

Decide what item of clothing you want to teach your child to take off first, then put on (this is the easiest order). Teach one item at a time. The following are ways of developing dressing skills:

- Backward chaining would be a useful method to teach putting on items of clothing, e.g. putting on trousers:
    - help your child to put trousers on, as far as the knees; the child pulls trousers up independently;
    - help him/her put trousers on as far as the ankles; the child pulls up trousers independently;
    - put one leg in; the child continues;
    - the child is shown how to lay trousers out and put them on;
    - the child sits and independently puts trousers on.
- Encourage your child to sit on the floor with something behind, e.g. wall, settee, when dressing.
- Practise doing fasteners on dolls with large buttons, zips and Velcro, doing fastenings on Mum's and Dad's clothes.
- Practise with clothes which are much too large first; play dressing-up games with large clothes.
- Practise dressing at weekends or when there is more time.

- Use T-shirts/sweatshirts with a logo/design on the front to help with the orientation of clothes.
- Praise your child when he/she is trying to dress independently.

Older children

- Mark shoes with a code to show which is right or left, e.g. stick half a smile shape or half a football shape in each shoe, which your child has to match together in order to put his/her shoes on the right feet.
- Place your child's clothes on the bed in the order they are to be put on to help him/her dress more independently.
- Use a cue card to encourage dressing without help.

| Trousers | T-shirt | Trainers | Jumper |

- Time how many minutes it takes to dress and make a competition to see if your child can improve the time (taking care not to cause anxiety).
- Clothes need to be considered carefully to enable the child to have credibility with his/her peers.
- Consider how fashions can be adapted to make dressing easier:
  - Adapt clothes, e.g. cut the school tie and join with Velcro or elastic; adapt cuffs by putting in elastic to allow the hand to fit through; put Velcro behind a button.
  - Wear polo shirts, jumpers with logos to help orientation, jumpers with raglan sleeves; wear a belt with a magnetic buckle.
  - Use 'elastic shoelaces' which allow shoes to be laced at home and slipped on and off at school. 'Coiler' shoelaces are elastic based laces which do not require tying. The shoe is laced and the lace coils, to keep it in place (available from 'Homecraft', tel: 01623 757555). A long shoehorn can also help with putting on shoes.

Personal care

Toileting:

- Dress your child in clothes that are easy to pull up and down.
- Make sure he/she can sit safely on the toilet with feet on a step if necessary.
- Use wet wipes for cleansing after using the toilet.
- Consider the use of cue cards for children who find it difficult to establish a toileting routine.

| Check that you are clean | Wash your hands | Check in the mirror |

Personal appearance:

- Encourage younger children to use a long mirror to develop awareness of body size and shape.
- Encourage checking in a mirror before leaving the house; put a written checklist near the mirror, e.g.:

> ✓ shirt tucked in
> ✓ hair combed
> ✓ zip fastened
> ✓ underwear not showing
> ✓ collar tucked in

Developing eating skills

Younger pupils often dislike foods with variable textures, find it difficult to manipulate cutlery, preferring to finger-feed, and may have poor oral skills which make chewing more difficult.

- Give a packed lunch, which can be eaten with fingers.
- Practise using spoons, knives and forks in play situations, e.g. by spooning sand, cutting playdough, clay, etc.
- Practise feeding at home:
  - spoon yogurt;
  - give food which can be stabbed with a fork;
  - use a knife to slice soft foods, e.g. banana, progressing to harder foods;
  - use a spoon and fork with soft foods;
  - use a knife and fork.

- Some children with co-ordination difficulties may not tolerate different textures of food easily; introduce new textures gradually.

- Some children may prefer food at particular temperatures; introduce new temperatures of food gradually.

- Some children may not like a variety of foods on one plate; allow for this and gradually try to extend the types of food on the plate.

- Use Dycem or a damp tea towel to stabilise dishes.

- Moulded cutlery helps place fingers in the correct place.

- Adapted cutlery with built-up handles can help pupils with weak wrists.

Visual timetable: KS1

Visual timetable: KS2

Monday	Tuesday	Wednesday	Thursday	Friday
Literacy	Maths	History	Maths	PE
Maths	RE	Maths	Literacy	Maths
Break	Break	Break	Break	Break
Literacy	Geography	Literacy	Music	Literacy
ICT	French	Science	PE	Art
Lunch	Lunch	Lunch	Lunch	Lunch
Geography	Science	ICT	Geography	French
D&T	History	Art	History	Science

Professionals involved

Professional	Personnel	Contact number
Special needs adviser		
Educational psychologist		
Physical Disability Service		
SENSS		
Visually Impaired Service		
Hearing Impaired Service		
SENCO		
Education welfare officer		
Asthma support nurse		
School nurse		
Physiotherapist		
Occupational therapist		
Speech and language therapist		
Social worker		

Useful contacts

Brain Gym	www.braingym.org
British Dyslexia Association 98 London Road Reading Berkshire RG1 5AU Tel: 0118 966 2677	www.bda-dyslexia.org.uk
Contact a Family (CAF) 209–211 City Road London EC4 1JN Tel: 020 7608 8700	www.cafamily.org.uk
Down's Syndrome Association 155 Mitcham Road London SW17 9PG Tel: 020 8682 4001	www.downs-syndrome.org.uk
Dyspraxia Foundation 8 West Alley Hitchin Hertfordshire SG5 1EG Tel: 01462 455016	www.dyspraxiafoundation.org.uk
Handwriting Interest Group 5 River Meadow Hemingford Abbots Huntingdon Cambridgeshire PE28 9AY	www.handwritinginterestgroup.org.uk
Hypermobility Syndrome Association 15 Oakdene Alton GU34 2AJ	www.hypermobility.org
National Autistic Society 393 City Road London EC4 1NG Tel: 020 7833 2299	www.nas.org.uk

Resources

Resources to support fine motor development

Category	Item	Approx. cost	Supplier
Scissors	Table top block scissors	£29.95	Rompa
	Dual control training scissors (L & R)	£5.95	Taskmaster Ltd
	Longloop whole hand scissors (L & R)	£4.75	As above
	Press down scissors	£7.95	As above
	Easy grip loop scissors	£5.25	As above
	Small easy grip loop scissors	£3.95	As above
	Fiskar Squeezers	£39.95 (for 12)	NES Arnold
	Fiskar Junior scissors (L & R)	£2.99	As above
	Fiskars for kids	£2.99	As above
	Self-opening scissors (L & R)	£7.34	Smith and Nephew Homecraft
'Cutting skills'	Programme to support cutting skills	£9.99	LDA
Pencil grips	Tri-go	£4.95 (for 10)	Taskmaster Ltd
	Stubbi (same as Stetro)	£3.95 (for 10)	As above
	Ultra grip	£5.45 (for 10)	As above
	Comfort grip	£3.25 (for 10)	As above
Dycem	Non-slip material on roll	£12.95 for 2 m	Smith and Nephew Homecraft
	Self-adhesive strips (to make non-slip rulers)	£3.72	As above
Sloping writing surface	Write Angle	£34.00	Philip and Tacey Ltd
	Writestart Desk	£35.00	LDA
	Posture Pack	£50.00	Backinaction Tel: 020 7930 8309
Pencils	Writestart pencils	£3.99 (for 12)	LDA
	Berol Hand hugger pencils	£5.50 (for 12)	NES Arnold
	Noris Triplus Triangular pencils	£5.99 (for 12)	As above
Pens	Berol Handhugger fibre tip pen	£9.99 (for 36)	As above
	Rubber barrel pens with varying flow/resistance		Most stationery shops
Practice paper	Tram-line handwriting paper (10 mm/6 mm)	£6.00 (500 sheets)	Hope Education
	Learn to Write and Space	£3.00 for 2 pads	As above
Handwriting programmes	'Write from the Start' by Teodorescu & L Addy	£29.95	LDA
	'A Hand for Spelling' by Charles Cripps		As above
Compass	Safe drawing compass	£8.25 (for 10)	Hope Education
Rulers	Alligator easi grip ruler	£13.95 (for 6)	As above
	Make your own using 2 × 1 cm strips of self-adhesive Dycem		
Reading aid	Reading Helper		Reading Helper Tel: 0113 257 7796
	Reading Window		LDA
Construction toys	Stickle bricks	£17.85	Yorkshire Purchasing Organisation
	Magnetic blocks	£27.80	
	Clic	£45.75	
Writing aid	Clicker 4		Crick Software Ltd

Resources to support PE

Beanbags	Available as rabbits, frogs and turtles	£9.95 (for 6)	NES Arnold
Balls	Spordas spider ball	£4.95 each	NES Arnold
	Koosh ball	£21.95 (for 6)	As above
	Tail ball	£2.95	As above
	Floater ball (large, light slow moving)	£4.95	As above
	Plus balls (inflatable paper balls – very slow)	£16.95 (for 20)	As above
	Easy Katch ball (tendrils)	£2.99	Hope Education
	Rubber flex Graballs	£16.95 for 6	As above
Cones	Set of cones (alphabet or number)	£25.56	As above
	Marked cone drill set (with worksheets)	£24.95	
Basketball	Adjustable height basketball net	£45.95	Yorkshire Purchasing Organisation
	Little Sure Shot	£39.95	Hope Education
Bowling alley	(easy storage)	£75	As above

Resources to support food technology

Non-slip mats	Dycem mats available individually or on a roll	Approx £5 each or £14 for 2 m roll	Smith and Nephew Homecraft
Holding equipment	Clyde grater, scraper & spike – to hold vegetables, and integral grater on a non-slip base	£23.00	As above
	Food preparation system – for use by those who have difficulties gripping	£45.00	As above
	Pan handle holder – to prevent the pan moving while stirring with one hand	£10.00	As above
	Kettle tilt – to assist with pouring	£20.00	As above
Alternative cutting equipment	Rapid chopper – a single hand operated chopper with an integral blade	£11.00	As above

Resources to support recording skills

Spelling	'An Eye for Spelling' by Charles Cripps		LDA
	Starspell (computer program for PC)		Inclusive Technology
	'Toe by Toe' by Keda & Harry Cowling		Toe by Toe (ISBN 0952256401)
Number	'Numbershark' (for PC)		Inclusive Technology
	'1–100' (for PC)		SEMERC
Drafting	'Write:Outloud' (talking word processing)		Don Johnston
	'Co:Writer' (word prediction)		As above
Planning	'Kidspiration' (notes, mind maps)		SEMERC
	'Inspiration' (similar but for older pupils)		As above
	'Draft:Builder' (as above)		Don Johnston

Resources to support social skills

Home/school	'Socially Speaking' (book/game)		LDA

Prices correct as at May 2004

Suppliers

Address	Tel. number/neb/email	Equipment
Atkinson Vari-tech Ltd Unit 4 Sett End Road Shadsworth Blackburn Lancashire BB1 2PT	01254 678777 www.vari-tech.co.uk	Variable height tables to support Art, D&T, ICT
Crick Software Ltd Crick House Boarden Close Moulton Park Northampton NN3 6LF	0845 121 1691 www.cricksoft.com/uk	Writing aid
Don Johnston Special Needs	01925 256500 www.donjohnston.co.uk	ICT, hardware and software
Economatics (Education) Ltd Epic House Darnall Road Sheffield S9 5AA	0114 281 3311 www.economatics.co.uk	QX3 Computer Microscope
Hope Education Hyde Buildings Ashton Road Hyde SK14 4SH	0845 120 2224 www.hope-education.co.uk	Fine motor and PE equipment, adapted furniture
Inclusive Technology Ltd Gateshead Business Park Delph, Oldham OL3 5BX	01457 819790 www.inclusive.co.uk	ICT equipment and software
LDA Duke Street Wisbech Cambridgeshire PE13 2AE	01945 463441 www.ldalearning.com	Fine motor equipment
NES Arnold Findel House Excelsior Road Ashby Park Ashby de la Zouch Leicestershire LE65 1NG	0845 120 4525 enquiries@nesarnold.co.uk	Fine motor/PE equipment

Nottingham Rehab Supplies Novara House Excelsior Road Ashby Park Ashby de la Zouch Leicestershire LE65 1NG	0845 120 4522 www.nrs-uk.co.uk	Adapted furniture, fine motor/ PE/food technology equipment
Philip and Tacey Ltd North Way Andover SP10 5BA	01264 332171 www.philipandtacey.co.uk	Desktop writing aid
Rompa Goyt Side Road Chesterfield S40 2PH	0800 056 2323 sales@rompa.com	Scissors
SEMERC Granada Learning Ltd Granada Television Quay Street Manchester M60 9EA	0161 827 2927 www.semerc.com	ICT equipment and software
Smith and Nephew Homecraft Ltd PO Box 5665 Kirby-in-Ashfield Nottinghamshire NG17 7QX	01623 721000 homecraft.sales@ smith-nephew.com	Adapted furniture, fine motor/ food technology equipment
Taskmaster Ltd Morris Road Leicester LE2 6BR	0116 270 4286	Pencil grips, scissors, fine motor equipment
Toe by Toe 8 Green Road Baildon Shipley BD17 5HL		Reading Manual
Yorkshire Purchasing 41 Industrial Park Wakefield WF2 0XE	01924 824477 www.ypo.co.uk	Fine motor/PE equipment

David Fulton Publishers

Improve your support for pupils with SEN with other books in this series...

The books in this series gather together all the vital knowledge and practical support that schools need to meet specific special needs. Information is simply explained and clearly sign-posted so that practitioners can quickly access what they need to know. Each book describes a specific area of special educational need and explains how it might present difficulties for pupils within the school setting. Checklists and photocopiable forms are provided to help save time and develop good practice.

Supporting Children with Behaviour Difficulties

£10.00 • Paperback • 64 A4 pages • 1-84312-228-6 • July 2004

Supporting Children with Co-ordination Difficulties

£10.00 • Paperback • 64 A4 pages • 1-84312-227-8 • July 2004

Supporting Children with Fragile X Syndrome

£10.00 • Paperback • 64 A4 pages • 1-84312-226-X • July 2004

Supporting Children with Speech and Language Difficulties

£10.00 • Paperback • 144 A4 pages • 1-84312-225-1 • July 2004

Supporting Children with Medical Conditions

£20.00 • Paperback • 144 A4 pages • 1-84312-224-3 • May 2004

Supporting Children with Epilepsy

£10.00 • Paperback • 64 A4 pages • 1-84312-223-5 • May 2004

Supporting Children with Dyslexia

£10.00 • Paperback • 48 A4 pages • 1-84312-222-7 • July 2004

Supporting Children with Down's Syndrome

£10.00 • Paperback • 48 A4 pages • 1-84312-221-9 • May 2004

Supporting Children with Cerebral Palsy

£10.00 • Paperback • 48 A4 pages • 1-84312-220-0 • May 2004

Supporting Children with Autistic Spectrum Disorder

£10.00 • Paperback • 64 A4 pages • 1-84312-219-7 • May 2004

Supporting Children with Asthma

£10.00 • Paperback • 48 A4 pages • 1-84312-218-9 • May 2004

ORDER FORM

Qty	ISBN	Title	Price	Subtotal
	1-84312-218-9	Supporting Children with Asthma	£10.00	
	1-84312-219-7	Supporting Children with ASD	£10.00	
	1-84312-228-6	Supporting Children with Behaviour Ds	£10.00	
	1-84312-220-0	Supporting Children with Cerebral Palsy	£10.00	
	1-84312-221-9	Supporting Children with Down's Syndrome	£10.00	
	1-84312-222-7	Supporting Children with Dyslexia	£10.00	
	1-84312-223-5	Supporting Children with Epilepsy	£10.00	
	1-84312-226-X	Supporting Children with Fragile X Syndrome	£10.00	
	1-84312-224-3	Supporting Children with Medical Conditions	£20.00	
	1-84312-227-8	Supporting Children with MCDs	£10.00	
	1-84312-225-1	Supporting Children with S&L Difficulties	£10.00	
	1-84312-204-9	David Fulton Catalogue	FREE	

Postage and Packing: FREE to schools, LEAs and other institutions.
£2.50 per order for private/personal orders.
Prices and publication dates are subject to change.

P&P

TOTAL

Payment:

☐ Please invoice *(applicable to schools, LEAs and other institutions)*

☐ I enclose a cheque payable to David Fulton Publishers Ltd *(include postage and packing if applicable)*

☐ Please charge to my credit card *(Visa/Barclaycard, Access/Mastercard, American Express, Switch, Delta)*

card number

expiry date

(Switch customers only) valid from   issue number

Please complete delivery details:

Name: ....

Organisation: ....

....

Address: ....

....

....

....

Postcode: ....

Tel: ....

Email: ....

☐   Please add me to your email mailing list

Send your order to our distributors:

**HarperCollins Publishers
Customer Service Centre
Westerhill Road • Bishopbriggs
Glasgow • G64 2QT**

Tel. 0870 787 1721

Fax. 0870 787 1723

or order online at
www.fultonpublishers.co.uk

DEMCO